Parenting Well in a Media Age
Keeping Our Kids Human

Parenting Well in a Media Age

Keeping Our Kids Human

Gloria DeGaetano

PERSONHOOD PRESS

Parenting Well In a Media Age

Note:
The chart, Scientific vs. News Reports of the Effect of Media Violence on
Aggression, is used with permission from The John Hopkins University Press.
The chart appeared on page 151 of *Kid Stuff: Marketing Sex and Violence to America's
Children*, edited by Diane Ravitch & Joseph P. Viteritti, published by The John
Hopkins University Press. Many thanks to The John Hopkins University Press
for this kind permission.

Published by
Personhood Press
P.O. Box 370
Fawnskin, CA 92333
800-429-1192
personhoodpress@att.net
www.personhoodpress.com

ISBN: 1-932181-12-1

Book and Cover Design by Wayne Turner

Printed in the United States of America

To Ida Barbara and Albert Bernard,
with deep gratitude and much love.

For Matthew and Adam,
your authentic expression encourages my own.

Acknowledgments

I am extremely grateful to my colleagues at the Parent Coaching Institute, particularly Janet Heverling, Lynn Faherty, and Michelle Strickland who contributed their expertise on media and children and gave generously of their time and energy. I thank Susan Horst, Sally Kidder Davis, Mary Scribner, Chris Christensen, Robin Rousselle, Rachel Eden, Bridgid Normand, and Jennifer Mangan, for their on-going support. I also very much appreciate the support of the following individuals:

Friends, Anne Juhlian, Wendy Johnson, and Lynn Haney offered many kindnesses, along with honest appraisals and gentle nudges.

My mother, brother, Al, and sister, Barbara served as "guardians of the process," celebrating each milestone with continued, often much-needed, encouragement.

Dr. Craig Anderson, Dr. Jane Healy and Michael Medved took time away from their important work to review the manuscript under tight deadlines.

Dr. Diane Dreher, supportive friend and mentor, wrote a wise Foreword to the book, supporting my vision in her usual kind and caring way.

The parents, parent coaches, and family advocates that I interviewed offered me their time and wonderful ideas without hesitation.

Adam Thomas gave me on-going, friendly camaraderie along with many useful opinions that made important differences.

Matthew Thomas, senior editor, generously provided insightful ideas and necessary organizational changes.

My husband, David Moore, lent his most fascinating mind once again to a project of mine, making the arduous task of writing yet another surprising, delightful adventure.

CONTENTS

Foreword

America is a nation founded on dreams—the dream of democracy affirmed by the *Declaration of Independence*, which has evolved over the years, becoming more inclusive with emancipation, women's suffrage, and the civil rights movement. From the beginning, Americans have defined themselves as citizens, actively committed to the realization of their dreams and the education of their children, which Thomas Jefferson saw as the foundation of our democracy. But our changing technology has dramatically transformed how we see our families and ourselves. In a profit-driven culture that substitutes products for the process of active participation, the citizen has become a consumer.

Parenting Well in a Media Age articulates the challenges of parenting in such a culture—a culture Gloria DeGaetano refers to as an "industry-generated culture." Offering new hope to parents and educators, Gloria DeGaetano presents powerful strategic advice. As a parent, nationally-recognized media literacy expert, and founder of the Parent Coaching Institute, she writes from years of experience, demonstrating how the industry-generated culture has produced a systemic imbalance that has led to diseases of body, mind, and soul. Drawing upon the latest scientific research, DeGaetano explains how excessive exposure to screen media distorts brain development, impacting children's and teens' abilities to develop healthy relationships or learn essential lessons in school.

Although our country produces many useful consumer goods, our invasive advertising and obsessive product orientation have usurped our children's dreams and hijacked their imaginations. In one of the saddest examples in this book, a third grade teacher says that many of her students cannot play creatively. Unable to make up their own stories or imagine their own futures, they can only repeat stories about cartoon characters or the exploits of the latest action hero. What will become of a country when its young people can no longer dream?

Moving from the industry-generated culture to the living values within and around us, *Parenting Well* provides positive alternatives to the compulsive consumerism that litters our lives. The book tells us how to transform our homes and simplify our lives to make time for appreciative conversation, reflection, interaction, and introspection. Each chapter offers practical solutions, strategies that *work*, supported by research and reinforced by real life stories of parents who have rediscovered the sacred joys of parenting. We learn how to declare our independence from mindless mass conformity to reconnect with our inner lives, our love for our children, and our own deepest values, producing positive change in our families and our culture.

Resisting the industry-generated culture requires the courage to be ourselves. In *Parenting Well*, Gloria DeGaetano shows us how to live more courageously and more joyously, embracing our daily choices as creative acts. In so doing, we can overcome the artificial values that have infected our culture and renew our vocation as parents, helping our children develop as healthy, creative human beings. By upholding human values instead of industry-generated counterfeits, we can reclaim our essential role as citizens, restoring vital balance to our lives, our families, and our collective future.

Diane Dreher, Ph.D.
March 2004

Introduction

Like cowboys making up songs around the campfire,
we hanker to create the culture we inhabit.
Michael L. Umphrey[1]

You may have heard about the groundwater pollution in the desert town of Hinkley, California, popularized by the movie *Erin Brockovich*. High levels of the carcinogen chromium 6 were dumped into the groundwater around Hinkley and absorbed into the aquifer that provided the town's drinking water. This contributed to the sickness or death of many adults and children who lived in the area. Doctors treated each ill person as if the cause of their declining health was *in* the person. But the real problem was a collective, environmental one. The real problem was *outside* of the people because the water essential to their survival and health was poisoned. For those who had already ingested too much of the carcinogen, there was often little that could be done. And, until the toxins were removed from their drinking water, there was no way to prevent others from becoming ill.

It's often said that "It takes a village to raise a child." To be effective parents, we have to rely upon resources outside of ourselves—social, cultural, and spiritual resources are necessary to support, strengthen, and renew us in our parenting. We may liken these collective resources to an aquifer. We each sink a personal "parenting well" into this collective "aquifer." From it we draw insights and impetus for the most important job on the planet. We naturally expect this aquifer to be free of toxins. But in the

United States today, the aquifer that our parenting wells draw on is being poisoned. Good intentions and caring actions for our children (and for ourselves) are falling short. We can read all the latest parenting books, search for answers from experts on the Internet, and work hard supporting our kids, but ultimately, that's not enough. Nowadays, a significant external force affects our parenting. Until we understand and abate that force, we will lose our power to parent well.

That force is mass culture. It exists outside of ourselves, yet surrounds us and our kids. Mass produced entertainment, like TV, movies, music, radio, video games, computer software, along with mass produced toys, clothes, lunch boxes, and countless other accessories, form a larger culture that we inhabit but don't create. This culture, manufactured for a market, is actually a huge industry that combines advertising conglomerates, media entertainment multi-nationals, and global corporations. I call it an industry-generated culture. The messages of these huge companies are delivered to the masses through mass media. So I refer to our society as a media age. An industry-generated culture relies on the media for its existence. It couldn't exist without a mass delivery system. Screen technologies, particularly, form a historically unprecedented, massive transmission engine, enabling industry-generated messages to reach millions simultaneously.

Screen machines bring mixed blessings. Don't get me wrong. I love my computer and can't imagine how anyone wrote books without them. I can remember when librarians, instead of scanning a barcode with a computer, had to write a number inside your books before they were checked out. What do librarians do now with all their free time? Computers have brought us many gifts.

So has our networked society. When an earthquake struck the Pacific Northwest, my oldest son called me from Los Angeles to ask if I was OK before the tremors had even stopped. He had heard about the earthquake on television—*as it was happening.* The other day a friend of mine had to hang up quickly from our phone call to take another one. Three minutes later I got a note of apology from her through e-mail. These examples of instantaneous communication made possible by modern-day screen machines demonstrate how screen technologies can draw us closer together as humans. And, of course, when the industry-generated culture works for us, we can parent well. For instance, when we globally gather around the electronic hearth to share the Olympics, a documentary by Ken Burns, or a newscast about an important world event, who cannot be immensely grateful for the potential of television to inform? Likewise, when we see an inspiring film, get alerted to new music, or listen to a radio conversation that causes us to think differently, who cannot be excited about all the wonderful richness of diversity and creativity available to us? Too bad that's not always the case.

The darker side of the industry-generated culture delivered through screen machines means that the messages they deliver are not always compatible with what we want as parents for our children. This type of culture is new to humans, so parenting in it is new as well. And it's tricky. Even if we turn off the televisions in our own homes and rigorously monitor video, movies, video games and computer usage, our kids still live and breathe in an industry-generated culture.

Most of society expects parents to fight industry-generated messages alone. Bill O'Reilly, host of the Fox News Channel's immensely popular *The O'Reilly Factor,* writes in his book *Who's Looking Out for You?,* "…effective parents will remove the TV's and computers from the kids' rooms. All media absorption should be done in public space. This is a dangerous world and the danger is now in the house. If the parent is really looking out for the kid, subversive material must be kept to an absolute minimum. Corrupting influences on children are everywhere, and parents must be full-time firefighters…The demons, the exploiters want your kids. You must look out for them. Fight hard." [2] O'Reilly's parental advice makes sense. Many parents I work with don't put TVs or computers in their children's bedrooms. But we must question the underlying, unspoken assumption in his advice. Why do parents have to fight hard to impart their values to their kids? Should not the larger society support us? And shouldn't we expect to parent in a world without "corrupting influences everywhere?"

Ideally, we'd live in a larger culture that affirms the morals, values, attitudes, and behaviors we teach our children, a culture that affirms our parental voice. But we don't.

Parents find themselves in a "Catch-22." As a "self-regulating" industry, the industry-generated culture sets standards and affects wide-spread beliefs. It doesn't, however, bear responsibility for the effects of those standards and beliefs. The media industry will give plenty of lip service to ratings systems. Then it and its ally companies will intentionally market inappropriate content and a range of superfluous items to our youngsters. Their mantras, "It's up to parents to prevent their kids from seeing this stuff," and "Parents shouldn't buy it if they don't like it," are repeated incessantly. As parents strive to stay afloat and in control, they find themselves continually reacting to toxic messages, dealing with nagging kids, and contradicting corporate hucksters. Kay Hymowitz, an affiliate scholar with the Institute for American Values, reminds us that "parents need to do something they've never been required to do before perhaps at any time in history: deliberately and consciously counter many of the dominant messages of their own culture." [3]

If we had a relative living with us who frequently acted in anti-social ways, who said and did things that would damage our children, and who often contradicted what we told our children, and if we had to live with this relative because a mental institution was out of the question, how would we parent our kids in such an environment? It would demand far more from us than if we had a relative living with us that we could trust to help us out, someone who reliably reiterated our messages to our kids. Even though we may want to, we can't confine the industry-generated culture to a mental hospital. We have to address it, no matter what it requires from us.

Since the inception of TV and the varied screen forms that followed, a majority of the viewing public chose and continues to choose mindless entertainment, vicarious violence, and exploitative sexuality. Why? Instead of becoming the "radio of the airwaves," as initially intended, "inspiring and educating along with entertaining," much of television today highlights the sensational and trivializes the sacred about the human condition. Why do we stand for this (actually we are sitting for it five hours every night) when there is so much work to be done to solve our social problems and relieve human suffering? What would happen if much of those 1,825 hours every year we spend watching TV were spent with our children and in our communities creatively addressing the environmental crisis, teen suicide, crime, homelessness? Why are screen machines considered normal background noise seven hours and forty-four minutes each day for most American households when their content has little to do with the daily lives of the individuals watching, or not watching, as the case may be?

Screen technologies are peculiar inventions. They readily appeal to human beings' baser instincts. Sex and violence "sell" so well because as humans we are wired deep in our brains to be attracted to erotic visions and horrific images. Screen technologies can only "hook" people's thinking functions to the degree that the viewers actually want to think. Sensational content with the sole purpose to titillate can be habit forming, leading to lazy minds. Human beings, therefore, can become addicted to screen technologies in ways they can't to vacuum cleaners, toasters, or air conditioners. We must re-invent ourselves to be conscious in how we use screen technologies, or they will use us.

The industry-generated culture takes extreme advantage of our human vulnerability to screen technologies. One way corporations do this is through the intentional cross-advertising, targeted marketing, and product-placement in movies, TV programs, and video/computer games. Saturating children and youth with visual messages works. Thus, many personal interactions among the young are focused on market-driven distractions.

I agree with media critic Todd Gitlin when he states, "Youngsters' interest is what interests me. Interest is not only an intellectual but an emotional state. Popular culture absorbs a great deal of young people's attention and does so in a fashion that commands feeling." [4] Listening to our children as they interact on school playgrounds, tuning in on teens' slumber party conversations, or eavesdropping on their telephone calls, we would hear many references to a culture manufactured by an industry. Why aren't first graders talking about the latest artwork they drew or the poetry they composed? Why are they talking about the cartoon they watched before school and the TV program they must watch after school? Why are many teens today preoccupied with how closely their bodies match the male and female models in the magazines they read more than with their own creative process? Rather than being attentive to their own inner lives, their own creative expressions, and to the people who love them, too much of our children's and teens' attention is focused by corporate agendas. The industry-generated culture captures our kids' interests, often replacing their own inner voices.

As humans we are influenced by personal interactions, by societal institutions, and by the over-arching culture. Personal influences are direct and colored by various degrees of intimacy. We talk with someone over a cup of coffee and exchange an idea, get an insight, or make a decision because of that particular connection. Personal relationships contribute powerfully, for good or ill, to our growth as human beings. Because we are directly engaged emotionally, we can notice fairly quickly if the other person has our best interests at heart. With personal contact it is usually easy to discern if the influence is dangerous, benign, or neutral. It may take some time to discern if it's worth the effort to walk away from a particular personal influence. For instance, when we "grow out of a friendship" with someone, it can be difficult to break the ties. In a more extreme example, a woman in a domestic violence situation may take years to recognize and leave that harmful influence. No matter how unconscious we may become of the personal influences in our lives, however, they remain the ones we can control most directly.

Societal influences are those influences primarily coming from institutions and the standards, mores, and values communicated by institutions such as school, church, and community interactions. They are less obviously visible in our day-to-day routines than personal influences, but more directly observed than cultural influences. A minister, teacher, or federal court judge may interact personally in their professional role, yet at the same time interact from an impersonal distance, as they have the responsibility to uphold the standards and rules of the institutions they represent. These societal rules and standards are, in turn, shaped by and contained within the underlying cultural belief systems.

Cultural influences are more pervasive than personal or societal influences. In a sense, cultural influences are like the invisible air, always present, such a part of us that we seldom notice, yet powerful because they greatly impact how individuals think about themselves and each other. Cultural influences strongly impact the inner picture each of us holds of the world. This inner picture or mental model consists of deeply ingrained assumptions and generalizations that influence how we understand the world and our place in it. Mental models act as reference points for helping us develop a self-identity, both as individuals and as a group. With mental models we envision our future.

Henry Giroux, Professor of Secondary Education at Pennsylvania State University, observes that "culture is the primary terrain in which adults exercise power over children both ideologically and institutionally." [5] An industry-generated culture exercises enormous power over children. It also presents an ideology, that is, a way of thinking about the world. But it's very different from a people-centered culture. In older societies the collective voice of the people developed the social rules of behavior. Extended family members taught the young, so children were directly influenced by real people. Parents could count on the community of the adults around them to uphold the values they taught to their kids. There was built-in reinforcement of the parental voice. Without encroachment from an industry-generated culture, parents and children were encircled by a societal structure in harmony with their needs. Obviously, we can't go back to such a society. We must find a way, however, for parents to be better supported in directly influencing their children within a highly complex industry-generated culture, owned by global enterprises.

We can no longer rely on the social structure around us to reiterate our messages to our kids. In fact, one of our biggest challenges as parents today is that too many societal influences are corporate clones. Many public schools, for instance, beam Channel One into the classrooms. In doing so, these schools implicitly add their authority to the commercial ads for junk food and violent video games the kids see each day. We also have to be suspect of organizations which purport to exist mainly to support parents. The National PTA, for example, "which for more than a century has promoted the health of children, now lists Coca-Cola Enterprises as a 'proud sponsor.'"[6] The thinking behind this decision reflects the kind of thinking that in its outward appearance seems to help, but in actuality, thwarts parents. PTA President Shirley Igo told the *Washington Post*, "We really need [corporate sponsors]. Our budget is very thin and if we didn't have them, we wouldn't be able to develop new programs."[7] The national PTA has now appointed John Downs Jr., "the point man for Coke regarding the marketing of soft drinks. . .in schools," to serve as an at-large member on the National PTA's Board of Directors.[8]

It's sad that the national PTA has "bought in" to a common misunderstanding: Organizations that serve the public can't function apart from large corporations. The need for money is seen as a greater need than keeping a clear focus on the organizational purpose. What our children are starving for, and some literally dying for, are adult role models of strong purpose and vision. Adults who live their values serve as powerful motivators. But what adults do for money also motivates our kids.

Blurring the boundaries between a well-intentioned service organization and a giant corporation can be dangerous. An industry-generated culture is seeking what it can get *from* the people, rather than what it can give *to* the people. What it gives and how it gives is always based on the monetary profit it gains. Its insatiable desire sets us up as objects—things to be manipulated so that we will buy and consume. In a true culture created by people, not an industry with an agenda, the focus is on providing for the life of the community. In such a culture, people develop talents, learn skills, and make their communities better for the people who come after them. In their book *Where God Lives in the Human Brain*, Carol Rausch Albright and the late James Ashbrook define culture as "the system of information passed from one generation to the next, not by genetic inheritance but by teaching."[9] Today's industry-generated culture actually interferes with our being able to teach and pass on our deepest values because it promotes a superficial life, with addictions and despair likely outcomes for many. It cannot give us a life-promoting belief system to further the optimal development of future generations because it is not a culture of and for real people, but a culture of and for objects.

An industry-generated culture is, by its very nature, impersonal. It does not care. It does not know our kids and doesn't want to. It can't teach our kids patience or morality or help our children learn about themselves. Only we can do that. If the industry-generated mass culture replaces the basic function of culture in our lives, we are likely headed into increased family and societal dysfunction. We will lose control of what is known as the "symbolic constructs and rituals" that previously gave our lives meaning. For instance, parents and religions still preserve the symbolic meanings of many of our holidays such as Christmas and Hanukah, while the industry-generated culture promotes rampant consumerism. Along with the materialism, comes a forgetting about the true symbolism of these holidays. We don't want to be the last generation to remember that meaning.

Walter Wink, a respected theologian and commentator on modern life, explains how in an industry-generated culture, we can fall prey to a slow erosion of our humanity. "The modern individual stripped of the values, rites, and customs that give a sense of belonging to traditional cultures, is the easy victim of the fads of style...fostered by the communication media. At once isolated and absorbed into the masses, people live under the illusion that the views and feelings they have acquired by attending to the media are their own. Overwhelmed by the giantism of corporations...individuals sense that the only escape from utter insignificance lies in identifying with these giants and idolizing them as the true bearers of their own human identity." [10]

If we don't generate our own culture, we relinquish our human identity to an industry-generated culture. If that happens, we lose vitality for our parenting and hope for our children.

Parenting Well in a Media Age turns parental attention away from the industry-generated culture and back where it belongs, on ourselves and on our children. If we want to move forward with a supportive personally-generated culture, we have two major parental obligations. First, we must work intentionally to develop a mature relationship with the industry-generated culture. That means understanding how to mitigate its negative effects. Second, we must work consciously to meet core human needs, not only for children, but for ourselves as well.

Creating a personally-generated culture, that culture of the people so many of us long for, will take effort, determination and rigorous allegiance to what we truly believe. It means parents express their inherent spiritual power and creativity in the world in exciting new ways.

My greatest hope is that *Parenting Well* helps you rediscover or renew your own courage and strength. I believe that we all must recognize and confront the challenges inherent in rearing children in this industry-generated culture. That takes a lot of self-trust, confidence, even boldness. The late Neil Postman, a renowned educator who understood the impact of an industry-generated culture on children, gave us this insight: "Children are the living messages we send to a time we will not see." [11] Our "living messages" must live in a personally-generated culture. Together, we can create that culture for our children.

Gloria DeGaetano

March 2004

I
Today's Parenting Challenges

The media have become the mainstream culture in children's lives.
Parents have become the alternative. Americans once expected parents
to raise their children in accordance with the dominant cultural messages.
Today they are expected to raise their children in opposition to it.

Ellen Goodman[1]

Being a parent is a precious gift. When children enter our lives, the outpouring of love we feel can be surprising. We wonder, "How can I love someone so much?" At the same time, we can wonder "What happened?" since most of us are totally unprepared to go from thinking only of ourselves to thinking of our children 24/7. Children take up residence in our heads, as well as in our hearts...and our lives are forever changed.

While our love for our kids can ease many difficulties, it can't erase the fact that parenting today is often quite a struggle. In a highly technological, fragmented society such as ours, many parents I meet feel isolated, misunderstood, and confused. These are tough times in which to parent well. While parenting has never been easy, over the past century our role has certainly become more complex. It's a very different job description from that of our great-grandparents, grandparents, or even our parents.

How Parenting Has Changed

In the first half of the 20th century, parents raised their children in pretty much the same way they had been raised. Child rearing practices were modeled after their extended family and the practices of their immediate communities. Being a parent was simply something that one did—not something someone had to read a book about to understand how to do. The abundance of information about right or wrong child-rearing techniques, so prevalent today, did not exist. Very few agencies provided direct services to parents. And no one taught "parenting" skills. The word "parenting," along with the concept, had not yet come into use. These parents, even though living in an increasingly industrialized world, were largely tied to time-tested traditions when it came to rearing children.

The primary parental tasks in the early 20th Century included feeding, clothing, and sheltering children until they were able to support themselves, or until they left home through marriage. Since physical existence required more manual labor, leisure activities were at a premium. Choices on how to spend family time, for instance, were limited. There were always household chores to do, and often plenty of kids around to help out. Families were larger back then and children played a much bigger role in supporting the life of the family than they do today. As a young girl in the 1920s, my mother recalls Sunday church services and a community meal afterwards as the one time during the week that her large family gathered "for fun." The rest of the week was taken up with her studying and chores after school. Her parents, too, were busy with their gender-specific roles. As a coal miner, my grandfather worked long, arduous hours and my grandmother managed a household of seven children.

Yet within this structured schedule my mother has fond memories of aunts, uncles, and cousins dropping in during the week, talking with her, laughing, joking, bringing food, or spontaneously sharing a family dinner. My mom couldn't escape into her room to watch a video or play a Gameboy at the dinner table, as children can do today. She had to stay at the table and listen. Observing the adults interact from this close proximity, like all the other children of the era, she learned about adult rules, communication, and social expectations. Both parents and children benefited from this communal aspect of simpler living. Having extended family members around helped with parental responsibilities, while giving children opportunities to participate in personal interactions that parents couldn't always provide.

The developing field of psychology brought new theories about human development. John B. Watson, the pioneer of behaviorist psychology, offered this advice to parents in 1928:

"The sensible way to bring up children is to treat them as young adults. Dress them, bathe them with care and circumspection. Let your behavior always be objective and kindly firm. Never hug and kiss them. Never let them sit in your lap. If you must, kiss them once on the forehead when they say goodnight. Shake hands with them in the morning…Put the child out in the back yard a large part of the time. Build a fence round the yard, so that it can come to no harm. Do this from the time it is born…let it learn to overcome difficulties almost from the moment of birth…away from your watchful eye. If your heart is too tender, and you must watch the child, make yourself a peephole, so that you can see without being seen, or use a periscope."[2]

The Atlantic Monthly praised this guidance as "a godsend to parents."[3] I can imagine both my grandmothers, born and raised in the "old country" of Europe, one from Italy, and the other from Poland, shaking their heads at the absurdity of this so-called "advice." Being close to their extended family's inherent wisdom, they knew better. Like many new mothers in the 1920s and 1930s, my grandmothers would find Dr. Watson's counsel ridiculous. But advice like this did not reach many parents at this time. Radio was just emerging as a means of communication; television was not yet in American homes. And, there wasn't any compelling reason yet for parents to look for outside advice on how to parent. Accordingly, ideas from experts were often ignored.

By mid-century, however, the social landscape of America had changed. Families had endured the depression and World War II. During the war, women helped run the factories, gaining a new sense of independence and competence. A generation of men, fueled by the GI Bill, went to college, where they were exposed to new ideas. The demand for consumer goods, pent up from both the depression and the war, drove the production of a material abundance never before experienced. As families moved to the suburbs, extended families became fragmented. Nearby strangers replaced community ties. New parents discovered that they were largely on their own, and began to search for advice. By the late 1950s, they were ready to listen.

Led by Dr. Benjamin Spock, the movement of learning to parent from credentialed experts, instead of from close relatives, transformed parenting. Spock's ideas caught hold and ushered in a more "hands-off" policy of child-rearing. The pendulum swing went from controlling children to "being their friends." But conflicting theories and contradictory information emerged, leading to confusion, experimenting, and new challenges. This parent generation also wanted to give their children more than they had been given. And they wanted their children to have less responsibility than had been forced on them. Over-indulgence joined permissiveness as the touchstones for being "good parents."

During the 1950s and 1960s, another fundamental change occurred in the nature of parenting that would affect us profoundly in our modern day. In 1959, the word *parenting* entered the dictionary. It identified an increased involvement with and commitment to one's children. Parenthood, a word whose origins go back to 1856, was the way parents defined their role in the first part of the century. Parenthood, a noun, connoted a state of being. Parenting, both a noun and a verb, defined a way of doing.[4] Parent educator and writer Polly Berrien Berends points out that "the word, parenting...turns parenthood, which is a state and stage of adulthood, into a verb and makes it into something that's done to the child as if it's the parent who causes the child to be human."[5] Diverse child rearing theories fueled the notion of parenting, and the state of being a parent became more and more a list of activities that parents did for their kids.

The parental job description grew from supplying basic needs, to giving the best of material things, meeting children's emotional and psychological needs, and providing them with quality education. During the 1970s and 1980s, participation in their children's socialization became a part of the parental task list. This meant making sure young children have "play dates" with peers, and older kids go to the right amount of birthday parties, school outings, sports events, etc., along with all the transportation required.

Today, we can include on our parental "to do" list finding the best schools for our kids, choosing childcare for infants and preschoolers, after-school care for elementary age kids, and making sure our teens are where they should be after school. We also have to teach them about and protect them from drugs. We have to provide relevant sex education. With the emergence of sexually transmitted diseases, especially AIDS, parental worries increased. With so many forms of screen entertainment, our responsibilities have also come to include monitoring children's use of television, videos, and video games. With the proliferation of computers, it now means making sure that our kids are computer literate, so they won't be "left behind." At the same time, we have to make sure they are protected against pornography, cyber stalking, and cyber bullying. With the widespread labels ADD or ADHD and the use of prescription drugs to treat children, many parents must work with schools and authorities to determine what is really "wrong with" their kids. And, post 9/11, we can add new dilemmas such as explaining terrorism to tots.

Modern-day parental tasks and responsibilities are indeed mind-boggling. Yet, on top of all of this, we face some very specific challenges that are present simply because we parent within an unsupportive culture.

Challenges Specific to Our Time

The negative elements of an industry-generated culture have always in some way been a concern to parents. What about parents' reactions to Elvis' seductive hip-swaying in the 1950s? Or the shock of Madonna's fashion sense in the 1980s? Parents have always voiced their opinions about the ever-changing "pushing of limits" so integral to the industry-generated culture. This is to be expected. There are significant distinctions today, however, that need to be clearly understood in order to be productively addressed.

Challenge #1: Global conglomerates influence behaviors and attitudes on an unprecedented scale.

In the '50s ten year-olds were not being sold Elvis but by the '80s little girls were dressing like Madonna. Over the years multi-national companies have increased their hold on our kids. Judith Rubin, writing in *Mothering*, reminds us that "marketing professionals cross-reference, cross market, and cross-pollinate products and entertainment. By intentionally blurring the distinctions between products, entertainment, school curricula, and advertisements, marketers readily capitalize on young children's limited ability to differentiate between them. It's no accident that in the children's section of Barnes and Noble, the books starring such television-based characters as Blue, Arthur, and Clifford are displayed most prominently, while the classics get the cheap seats."[6]

This decision of book placement in a popular store chain is one example of how large businesses can be so influential on our kids and impact our parenting on a daily basis. When the people who create, produce, and disseminate the TV programs or movies also have a lot of reach into other sectors, such as bookstores, we are virtually surrounded by focused messages, driven by maximizing profit. In the past, media companies were not nearly as influential. In fact, in 1983, as many as fifty companies owned the majority of the media. By 2001, six companies owned and controlled global media production and dissemination.[7] Ted Turner, founder of CNN, ironically decries media's consolidation of power, "Media concentration is a frightening thing. It's owned more and more by Disney, General Electric...Westinghouse, which now owns CBS. You have two of the four major networks owned by people that have huge investments in nuclear power and nuclear weapons—both GE and Westinghouse." [8] Time Warner, the world's biggest media corporation, is also the second largest book publisher in the world, the largest music company, and the owner of many of America's leading magazines, including *Time, Fortune, Life, People, Money,* and *Teen Magazine.* And, along with TCI, Time Warner is the owner of television cable systems serving 47% of the American cable audience.[9] The merger of Time and AOL in 2000 opened even more pathways for mass dissemination with Internet users.

Rachel Eden, a mother of a five year old daughter, writing in an article, "Children's Creative Thinking in the Face of Commercialism," points out, "The late Herbert Schiller, noted author, professor, and authority on corporate power and the media, gets to the heart of what is really happening with corporate mergers. In a speech titled, 'The Corporate Packaging of the Public Mind,' Schiller explains that these mergers between corporate media systems create a 'corporate packaging' designed to play on our sensory perceptions and perpetuate an outlook and consciousness shaped by the images they present. This is carried out through the local mall filled with the same stores owned by one chain. Many schools align themselves with corporations in exchange for funding or supplies which brings commercialism directly into the daily lives of students. In essence, our children become conditioned by this homogenized intake and the messages being promoted 'are reinforced throughout the social order.'"[10]

Eden, a third-grade teacher, sees children's imagination eroding every day in her classroom. "I have students who can't come up with an idea for a story unless the current toy can be the main character. It isn't the isolated incidents that concern me but rather a continual inability of children to conjure up their own ideas without relying on what the media has presented to them. There are youngsters who cannot create a story unless it revolves around a TV character or superhero, whose lunch items are colorfully decorated with the latest craze from the box office or Burger King, whose entire outfit and matching backpack are walking commercials for some movie. These children are so immersed in Disney, Nickelodeon, and Nintendo that they no longer have access to their own images and creative imaginations. Instead they are limited to thinking in the images the media has provided for them."[11]

Mary Burke, a mother and child psychiatrist, worries about the replacement of the imagination with packaged media products. "This was recently made concrete to me when I set out to order a variety of character toys for my sand tray, I was appalled to find that the local sand-tray supplier only carried Disney characters! I could no longer find witches, princesses and heroes, only the Disney versions of Snow Whites's step-mother, Cinderella, and Aladdin."[12]

This "homogenized intake" pervasively influences our children. One Seattle mother of three children, calls it "Any Child USA." "Malls are Anywhere USA and our children become Any Child USA. Instead of our children being who they are, they now have the wants and needs of people who don't know them." By influencing on a mass scale, the industry-generated culture shapes attitudes and impacts our children's identities in profound ways.

Since it's shaping millions of children simultaneously, peer group pressures to conform increase as corporations get increasingly savvy in selling straight to our kids. Children, of course, have very real needs to fit in and to be like their friends. As we work diligently to help our youngsters develop their unique identity, we have to counter homogenized thoughts and behaviors our kids learn from their peer group, without ostracizing them from their peers. This is a tricky job. Trying to parent well within this framework raises a critical parental question that we all have to answer: Whose messages do we want to be most influential in shaping the emerging identity of our children—the messages from an industry-generated culture or the messages from parents?

Challenge #2: The erosion of community standards through the co-opting of social institutions.

The second major distinction between parenting today and parenting in the past is the erosion of community standards through the co-opting of social institutions. From the 1950s through the early 1980s, social institutions kept corporate intrusion to a minimum. Gary Ruskin, president of Commercial Alert, a non-profit dedicated to countering commercial messages, points out: "Junk food marketers, for instance, tried to invade schools, but for decades their presence was relatively insignificant... The curriculum of junk nutrition began in earnest in 1989, with the launch of Channel One, an in-school TV marketing program. Chris Whittle, Channel One's founder, had the ingenious idea of harnessing the schools to show daily twelve-minute TV broadcasts that included two minutes of ads. Since then, Channel One, now owned by Primedia, has been adopted by 12,000 schools. About eight million children watch its ads for

Pepsi, Mountain Dew, Hostess Twinkies, M&M's, Snicker's and the like."[13] We expect MacDonald's to be more interested in selling Happy Meals than they are concerned about our kids' health; we don't expect schools to ignore our kids health needs. When schools join to amplify corporate messages, they dismiss parental concerns.

The local communities of those eight million kids watching Channel One most likely have YMCAs, YWCAs, Boys and Girls Clubs, church organizations and intramural sports teams that give children messages about proper nutrition. In fact, most of the schools that show Channel One have well-developed sports programs, promoting optimal heath. Giving kids mixed messages makes life difficult for parents. Children and teens need the culture outside the home to be supportive of the family's priorities. For instance, in order for a child to change an unhealthy eating pattern into a healthy one, two main things need to occur. First, the child must internalize the positive messages. He or she needs to "take them in" and believe in them. Industry-generated messages for unhealthy food choices, though, are repeated so often in the child's environment, making it virtually impossible for the child to come to value the seemingly dissonant message from the parent wanting to instill healthy eating habits. The second thing that must happen after internalization is integration. This refers to making the new behavior one's own. This integration can't easily happen if a social institution like a school where the child spends so much time—a place he or she relies upon for positive direction and nurturing guidance—cannot be counted on to echo parental messages. How will kids adopt parents' healthy eating habits when so many of their friends at school are eating junk food?

It should give us pause to realize that despite the well-researched facts and enormous individual efforts on the part of parents, teachers, doctors, and other professionals, child obesity continues to climb. In 1988, the American Academy of Pediatrics issued a report which revealed that forty percent of youngsters ages five through eight exhibit one risk factor for heart disease. In 2003, they issued a policy statement saying that a television in a child's bedroom is a strong predictor of childhood obesity.[14] Other medical research indicated that at least forty percent of all children under the age of twelve are overweight, and another study found an increased risk of obesity and diabetes for every two hours of television watched daily.[15]

Countering children's health problems within an industry-generated culture and unsupportive social structures pushing opposing messages is just one example of this trying parental challenge. Whenever the local community doesn't align itself in the bests interests of children, we parents have more work cut out for us. This brings us an important question: How do we help our children intentionally choose what is in their best interests when the industry-generated culture and social institutions in our communities persist in urging them to make choices not in their best interests?

Challenge #3: Corporations market specifically to children and their inherent vulnerabilities with the intention of undermining parental authority and responsibility.

A third parenting challenge unique to our times is the corporate intention to undermine parental authority and responsibility. By intentionally driving a wedge between the parent and child over a specified product, parental concern becomes scorned and the product becomes glamorized, almost magical. Parents are seen as stupid and unfair. The child's peer group may as well have an umbilical cord tied directly to global conglomerates. Since children are inundated with seemingly important messages, corporations become significant authorities in children's lives. Marketers' successfully appeal to the child's state of "precritical naivete, that childhood state in which we take for granted that whatever the significant authority figures in our lives tell us to be true is indeed true."[16]

Sneaky business tactics often infiltrate our homes. PG-13 movies are sometimes advertised on television during shows designed for young children. Parents, thinking the shows benign, let their children watch, unaware of the offensive, tantalizing trailers that come on between the shows. Sony, for example, tried to advertise *The Fifth Element*, a violent PG-13-rated movie, on Nickelodeon.[17] And they probably would have, if they weren't "caught." In a detailed report the Federal Trade Commission found that film, videogame, and television companies, including Sony, were marketing violent entertainment to young children. In one of the hearings, "Senator John McCain read aloud a segment from a marketing report for one R-rated movie which said, 'it seems to make sense to interview 10 to 11 year-olds...In addition, we will survey African American and Latino moviegoers between the ages of 10 and 24.'"[18] Even though the industry has defined R-rated movies as "no one under seventeen admitted unless accompanied by an adult," it fails to follow its own self-imposed standard. "Condemning industry execs for warning parents and simultaneously wooing children, McCain pointed out that 'it is your responsibility to refrain from making much more difficult a parent's responsibility to see that their children grow up healthy in mind and body into adults who are capable of judging for themselves the quality or lack thereof of your art.'"[19]

Parents can't trust the movie industry's rating system. Teens going to PG-13 movies see bunches of inappropriate content. Strippers, lap dancing, and references to oral sex are common. "How does it feel to have your head in a congressman's lap?" says one Washington staffer to another in *Legally Blonde 2*. In *Laura Croft: Tomb Raider*, a woman starts to perform oral sex on her crime-fighting partner, then changes her mind and handcuffs him to the bed. *The Spy Who Shagged Me* "includes a comic scene of a naked woman inserting a homing device into the anus of. . .the man she just had sex with."[20] Since the movie industry thinks this type of content is appropriate for teens, parents must act as the "bad guys" and prevent their kids from seeing such stuff "when all the other kids get to go." Filmmakers know that as long as there are slumber parties and VCRs, or TVs in teens' bedrooms, many kids will see these types of movies, more than once, despite parent opposition.

Manufacturers of inappropriate toys even brag about their strategies for side-stepping parents. Stink Blasters, squeezable three-inch dolls, "designed to break wind up to 30,000 times on demand," are priced for young allowances. Most parents don't want these toys in their house. "But you know that only makes the kids want them even more," says Harold Chizick, director of marketing for Spin Master, the toys' manufacturer. "Kids love them, but the parents hate them. So we priced them as an impulse, lower-priced item, and the kids can make their own decision when purchasing them."[21]

That parents "hate" the toys, movies, or music the industry-generated culture feeds our kids is of utmost importance. It needs to make parents superfluous in order to market directly to children. Because a lot of parents give kids their own spending money and don't monitor every purchase the kids make, a lot of inappropriate stuff is bought. On one hand, we want to empower our kids, give them opportunities to make wise choices on their own. On the other hand, we also want to keep toxic influences to a minimum. Knowing what to do is often difficult, further eroding our confidence and making it easier for the kids to take advantage of our wavering.

We want our kids to become independent thinkers. Supporting their autonomy is critical to their optimal development. Decades of research in child and adolescent development shows that parents who help kids feel empowered to make their own decisions, also help their kids to become well-functioning adults. Richard Ryan and Edward Deci, social psychologists from the University of Rochester, have done seminal research on autonomy in humans since the 1970s. Their work points out that people will not try to change their behaviors unless they feel a certain degree of autonomy to make positive choices. Indeed, autonomy is seen as one of the main conditions for healthy social development and personal well-being.[22]

It's easy for parents to get tripped up here and "buy into" an untimely autonomy for kids. Because the industry-generated culture pushes youngsters to make decisions without their parents' permission at earlier and earlier ages, a lot of parents don't take into consideration the developmental appropriateness of making decisions without parental influence. Both advertisers and parents want to empower children. But for different reasons. Kay Hymowitz, in the article "The Contradictions of Parenting in a Media Age," describes how advertisers, in the post World War II era of greater parental permissiveness, were quick to promote empowerment of children by disempowering adults. "Advertisers knew that empowered children could make better consumers than dependent, compliant ones. . .One way that the media could hasten the empowerment of children was by reducing authorities, and parents especially, in the child-consumer's eyes. This was a project media 'creatives' undertook with a vengeance."[23]

The message to parents, reflected through the lens of the industry-generated culture is that they are ridiculously up-tight and stupid if they try to exercise any authority in relationship to their children. Unfortunately this attitude has been supported by many "experts." That leaves parents in a state of confusion about what their proper role is in relationship to their children. Hymowitz goes on to add, "Caught between their distaste for a coarse and degraded popular culture and their belief in a free flow of information, parents. . .are in a bind that makes them ill-equipped to deal with the new realities of contemporary childhood."[24]

Over the last few decades, our parental authority gradually weakened while advertisers gained strength by devising improved ways to entice kids to make choices without our approval. A key question involves reclaiming our appropriate authority in such an environment: How do we nurture our children's and teens' healthy autonomy within an industry-generated culture determined to undermine our authority and responsibility?

Challenge #4: Lack of relevant information and a pattern of disinformation keep parents in a state of confusion, unsure and unaware.

The fourth major challenge combines a lack of relevant information and a pattern of disinformation that keeps parents in a state of confusion. Corporations spend millions each day to guide our attention in specific directions—often leaving out critical information that would be important to us as parents. This "intentional omission habit" means we focus on what is given. We can forget that other ideas and other perspectives actually exist. A simple test of how this works is to see how clear you are on two important parental issues—the appropriate amount of screen time for children and the effects of media violence. How would you answer these questions?

Questions:

1.   What is the American Academy of Pediatrics (AAP) most recent recommendation on the amount of screen time for your children? Why did they change their initial recommendation? (Did you know that the AAP even has a clear recommendation?)

2.   What does research show about the impact of media violence on your kids?

Answers:

1. The AAP has had long standing recommendation of two to three hours per day of TV for children. Recently the AAP changed this to one to two hours of *all* screen time per day and *no* screen time for babies and children under the age of two. If you did not know this, you are not alone.[25] Most parents I meet are unaware that the AAP even has a recommendation. It was changed

because pediatricians could no longer ignore the latest brain research and its implications. Overuse of screen technologies has devastating effects on children's brain development. In fact, many doctors and other professionals think the AAP's recommendation not strong enough. Dr. Robert Hill and Dr. Eduardo Castro, authors of the book, *Getting Rid of Ritalin*, recommend no television before the age of five. Having conducted on-going research and investigation into the matter, they state in no uncertain terms, "We can say with confidence that excessive television, particularly in young children, causes neurological damage. TV watching causes the brain to slow down, producing a constant pattern of low-frequency brainwaves consistent with ADD behavior."[26]

This relevant information for parents of kids of all ages is not something that you will see on television, the most prominent avenue for keeping parents abreast of new breakthroughs. Sitcom characters will not address these facts. Cartoons, of course, avoid them, and even news programs do not report this information.

2. If you are unaware of the impact of media violence, again you are not alone, as most parents don't know the basic information that would help them make important daily decisions about TV, movie, and video game content. Unless you are searching for the scholarly studies you would not know that there are over 3,000 studies demonstrating the negative influence of media violence. Yet, there persists a major gap between what is known about the effects of media violence and the actual news reports about these effects. In the chart below you can see that "as the state of scientific knowledge supporting a significant and causal link between media violence and aggression grew stronger, news media reports actually grew weaker."[27]

Scientific vs. News Reports
of the Effects of Media Violence on Aggression

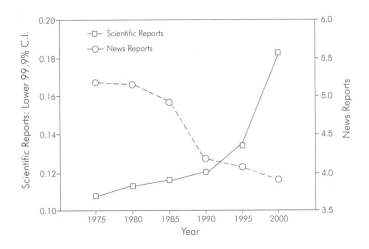

(Based on data reported in Brad J. Bushman and Craig A. Anderson, "Media Violence and the American Public: Scientific Facts Versus Media Misinformation," American Psychologist 56, no. 6/7 (2001): pp. 477-89.)

The amplified voice of the industry culture sends messages to parents that are counter to what the experts know, believe, and actually insist upon. Even when the information given parents seems valuable, the lens gets spotty and the importance of what parents must do becomes muddied. At times, while citing experts about the importance of play for young children's healthy development, for instance, the author ends with the notion that parents are too overwhelmed to do anything about the issue, too busy to follow the experts' advice. Here's "Just another thing" to add to the perennial parent to-do list.

Can you imagine an article in *Business Weekly* discussing what a bank president must do to make more money and then adding: "Poor bank presidents, how can we expect them to make money when they are too busy and overwhelmed?" If business consultants told CEOs they were too victimized to have the will to carry through on proven methods, they would be out of a job quickly. Anything less than a proactive, laser-like focus on what works is not acceptable when material productivity is at stake. In the parenting business, however, bewilderment and confusion are the status quo. And the gap in parent's knowledge about early childhood development continues to widen. *What Grown-ups Understand about Child Development* documents a survey done in 2000 and commissioned by the groups Zero to Three, Civitas Initiative, and Brio Corporation. It concluded that adults need better information "delivered in more accessible ways on understanding the depth of a baby's emotional life; theories on spoiling and spanking; expectations of young children at different ages; and choices of activities to promote development," including understanding the importance of play in a young child's life.[28]

Information about the need to control screen usage, protect kids of all ages from horrific violence, and to play more with youngsters, often gets no attention from the mainstream media. Yet, at the same time, Gameboys are marketed heavily to young children, cartoons and PG-13 movies contain unacceptable levels of violence, and children are beginning a "passive screen habit" at younger and younger ages.[29] What gets amplified is what sells. So many parents tell me, "I didn't know. If I knew this was harmful to my kids' brains or their best development, I wouldn't have done it." They often feel guilty for the choices they made. We parent with what information we have. If we have skewed or inaccurate information, that's what we use. We must be able to rely on the larger culture to give us the current information available, so that we can make the best informed choices possible. Tragically, that's denied us in an industry-generated culture.

The assumption that we are only consumers keeps important non-materialistic based information from entering parental psyches. Instead, an overload of trivia abounds. The advertising and media industries look at us and our children and see dollars, not souls. A crucial question we must answer both individually and as a society is: How do we parents get the relevant information we need to parent well when that information is not easily available through common mass media channels?

Challenge #5: An industry-generated culture turns mass attention to sensational and mindless content, while downplaying and often deriding analysis and other higher-level thought processes.

As this happens more people move away from demanding thoughtful programming, or voicing their outrage about sensational content. The industry-generated culture takes advantage and "pushes the envelope." With each year, we see increased levels of sexually explicit content. On television, for instance, in 1972, parents did not have to worry if their children tuned into *The Dick Van Dyke Show*. They knew Rob and Laurie Petrie would not be discussing their sex life.[30] Today words such as "bitch" as well as demeaning sexual references are common not only on sitcoms, but also in soap operas and MTV. Teen music abounds with misogynistic references and sadistic images. Several studies have shown that preschoolers watch more soap operas than they do children's programming, while kids ages eleven to twelve are the primary viewers of MTV.[31]

In this first decade of the 21st Century, entertainment content for both adults and kids has moved to a place that even ten years ago, our collective consciousness as a people could not have imagined. Children's cartoons, for instance, now average twenty five acts of violence per hour. The popular Power Rangers program contains over 200 acts of violence per hour![32] One mother of a five year-old boy recently told me she is "in agony" over having to curtail the Power Rangers re-runs for her son because of its high violence levels and at the same time, deal with her son being bullied in his kindergarten class for not knowing the show's characters. With increased escalation of violent content, come increased problems for parents and for schools as well.

"I'm clearly seeing an increasing number of kindergartners and first-graders coming to our attention for aggressive behavior," says Michael Parker, program director of psychological services at the Fort Worth Independent School District, near Dallas, Texas, which serves 80,000 students. The incidents have occurred not only in low-income urban schools but in middle-class areas as well. Says Parker: "We're talking about serious talking back to teachers, profanity, even biting, kicking and hitting adults, and we're seeing it in five year-olds." The alarming trend has been confirmed by Partnership for Children, a local child-advocacy group that has just completed a survey of child-care centers, elementary schools and pediatricians throughout Tarrant County, which includes Fort Worth and suburban Arlington. Ninety-three percent of the thirty-nine schools that responded to the survey said kindergartners today have "more emotional and behavioral problems" than were seen five years ago. More than half the day-care centers said "incidents of rage and anger" had increased over the past three years. "We're talking about children, a three year-old in one instance, who will take a fork and stab another child in the forehead. We're talking about a wide range of explosive behaviors, and it's a growing problem," says John Ross, who oversaw the survey.[33]

Video games also have increased in levels of violence. They've gone from *Pong* to games like *Grand Theft Auto III*, produced by Rockstar Games, which allows the player to shoot police officers up close in the face or as a distant sniper, or to set them on fire while hearing them scream as their flesh burns. Rockstar Games are also behind *Manhunt*, a game in which the player kills to vicariously satisfy "the Director," who whispers commands into the player's ear via an optional headset. This new dimension of the game can act to move a player beyond any reticence he or she may have in experiencing the "thrill" of maiming and destroying. The ultra-realistic violence sets *Manhunt* apart on the gaming scene, unnerving even those in the industry. "It's going to show people stuff they haven't seen in games before, but in slasher flicks," said Greg Kasavin, executive editor of GameSpot.com...There's a lot of blood, people getting strangled and killed with household weapons."[34] Although these games are marked "M for mature" several studies have shown that many children and youth who have video game systems in the home play such games regularly. A 2003 study of over 5,000 students, grades three-six, showed that most of the kids had played mature-rated video games. A 2002 study by the Minneapolis-based National Institute on Media and the Family reveals boys have easy access to "increasingly ultra-violent M-rated (mature) games." Their survey found that the popularity of video games among children and youth continues to increase.[35] It's critical for parents to pay attention to the ratings on these games. If you're not sure, play the game before you let your child see it. And watch where these games are advertised. Often gaming magazines, popular with junior high kids, will have full-page ads for ultra-violent games. Pick up a few of these magazines and look through them.

As entertainment content increases in "abnormality," it affects definitions of social "acceptability." The real world begins to look like the screen world, human behaviors change, and social norms adjust. Just as we are seeing increased levels of violence in our young children, we are also seeing this trend with our teens. Many professionals are concerned. "What strikes me as a researcher is what I see is an apparent increase in the brutality," says Ray Corrado, a criminologist at Simon Fraser University. Sibylle Artz, an expert in youth violence at the University of Victoria, agrees. "That seems to be a consensus among many people who deal with the youth directly," she says. "They all tell the same story, that they have this experience of this being more brutal, more extreme," says Artz. "When an attack is perpetrated, it doesn't stop when somebody's down." Corrado continues, "I've argued it might reflect the cultural norms of the last fifteen, twenty years, where video games and movies and music, even television, portray a level of violence that is really extraordinary." Artz agrees. "I believe that having the imagery constantly in front of them, [communicates] that it's fine to use weapons, clubs, action-hero type behaviors.... We are normalizing the use of violence in our efforts to sell goods."[36]

In 1992, film critic and social commentator Michael Medved, writing in his book, *Hollywood vs. America*, stated, "This simply cannot go on," in referring to the demise of cultural standards in the media industry.[37] He pointed out, "They don't begin to understand the values of the average American family, or the special concerns of the typical parents who worry about unwholesome influences on their children."[38] More than ten years after Mr. Medved's observation, most parents I meet are saying, "This simply can't go on." Yet, it does.

In addition to seeing much more explicit sexuality and horrific violence, kids are saturated today with bizarre images, a side-show circus reality, sometimes referred to as "the carnival culture." [39] For instance, on a recent MTV program, *Wildboyz*, a man voluntarily put eggs from a dead female salmon into his mouth and then the sperm from a live male salmon was placed on the eggs in his mouth. Since sixty-five percent of children, ages eight through twelve, have a television in their bedrooms and at least two million kids in this age range stay up until 2 a.m. watching TV each night, there is a good chance many might catch this show.[40] A young child watching this segment of *Wildboyz* gets introduced to salmon in a completely derogatory way. After watching this, it is difficult for the child to consider the salmon in any other context. When the child now reads about the salmon in a book emphasizing the mystery of its migration to spawn, or talks about the salmon in a science class at school, the demeaning image of salmon eggs being fertilized in a human mouth will be this child's reference point. Starting his instruction about salmon with such a gross image, how will he ever think of salmon in a more normal way?

Since visual mass media is filled with demeaning images, the cumulative effect of habitually paying attention to the distorted means that children grow up losing their "primal ability to wonder."[41] They can't easily get past the fascinating weirdness to appreciate mystery or beauty in life. There is logical reason for this when we understand the workings of the human brain. A mechanism inside the lower part (sometimes called the reptilian part) of the human brain actually makes us look at differences or distortions from what we would normally expect. This response is sometimes referred to as "the orienting response." That means humans orient to sudden changes or unusual disturbances or something "weird" in their environment. Since the unfamiliar could hurt or kill us, this quick reaction ability serves us well as a survival mechanism. If it is healthy it protects us from danger and works in harmony with upper brain processes to develop attention processes and thinking functions. When unhealthy, low brain processes can become like broken records—always looking for the next "thrill" in the form of external stimulation of some sort.

Humans can become addicted to an actual need for hyped stimulation. When this happens the brain's thinking capabilities remain under-developed and hyperactivity and impulsivity increase, making concentrated, focused attention more difficult. As youngsters watch four-five hours of television daily, their orienting response is continually activated by the change of images, on average, every three-five seconds.[42] Even in a room trying to do homework or play with the TV on as "background noise," children will orient to changes on the TV. In other words, they will look up and away from what they are doing, shifting their attention away from a self-directed activity and toward the flash of light of an image change on the television. Over time, serious problems can develop.

Children need to learn how to talk to themselves in a coherent way while engaging in an activity. This can't easily happen with the

TV interrupting continually. The constant shifting of the child's focus away from the self-directed activity and toward the TV means that the child's inner speech is continually disrupted and that the child's mental processing is aborted. Learning how to pay close sustained attention does not occur. The result is that low brain areas become more "in need" of stimulation and the cerebral cortex does not get practice in thinking things through methodically. Children's brains become disorganized and seek easy stimulation instead of the more effortful mental challenge. The natural and normal processes of thinking become tremendously difficult as the brain seeks hyper stimulation and avoids situations requiring deep thought.

The child now comes to value virtual violence over math homework, playing fast-paced video games instead of computer simulation games or board games like chess, and watching over doing. When producers of violence or pornography say, "We are just giving the people what they want," their statement holds truth. "The people" can be conditioned to want sensational content and gratuitous violence, especially when young brains are mutated during childhood and adolescence by continually attending to sensational visual content. The question presented to parents and anyone interested in children's welfare is: How can we stop the escalation of sensational, mindless content by the industry-generated culture if human brains are easily conditioned to seek it?

Challenge #6: An industry-generated culture pushes a "machine-like" view of the world, treats people as objects, amplifying the pseudo-need of a "quick fix" while avoiding the fact that we have human needs that must be met.

Our current, collective mindset stems from a way of thinking about the world that has been fundamental to Western culture for the last 300 years. But that mindset is changing. With new scientific discoveries we no longer view humans as machines, the prevailing image in the industrialized era. Now many scholars and professionals in science, theology, medicine, and sociology refer to humans from a more accurate perspective. Rather than being a "cog" in an impersonal wheel, this view of people is as a living system and an integral part of nature.

Living systems share common characteristics. For one, they are often unpredictable and outcomes are never guaranteed to be perfect—even when all the variables are controlled as tightly as possible. This makes us much more interesting than machines. Consider the case of CC, the first cloned cat. CC was named in honor of what cloning is all about—carbon copy. But when CC was born, geneticists were surprised. CC looked nothing like the cat from which it was cloned. Experts gave the reason for such an extreme variation: the random nature of living cells.

Another characteristic of living systems, including people, is an innate, natural intelligence. We experience the inherent intelligence of nature every spring when flowers burst out, when bright green buds appear on trees, and in some areas of the country, when deer come into our gardens to nibble the delectable buds. There are no questions about how the flowers came forth, why the green buds appeared, or how the deer know where to locate tasty treats. The innate intelligence of the natural world may be so evident and abundant that we don't consciously acknowledge it.

But this inner knowing is indeed fantastic. It distinguishes us remarkably from any machine—including computers, no matter how smart we program them to be.

Chris Christensen, a certified parent coach in Washington state, describes the differences between a mechanism and a living thing, showing how a living thing, as an interdependent system, expresses itself much differently than a mechanical thing.

> "The mechanism of a watch is carefully encased so small particles or liquids cannot damage constructed and calibrated parts which work together to provide an accurate knowledge of hours, minutes, and seconds. Just a bit of dust or grit in the gears could render a watch useless...it cannot adjust to major changes in its environment...A biological system is a living, evolving system of interdependent parts...The forest, for instance, has many interdependent parts. A forest fire may destroy many of them—for a time. Soon after a fire in a Pacific Northwest forest, for example, fireweed, grasses, dandelions, and insects appear. Salmonberry, blackberry, service berry and other shrubs gain a foothold. Alder trees follow, along with maple and other deciduous tress. Finally, coniferous trees return to dominate the landscape. The new forest is not identical to the old forest, though much is similar...a living, biological forest has been re-created."[43]

Humans are constantly evolving and adapting to their environment, much like forests. We replenish ourselves, too, when our needs are met. An industry-generated culture is not in the business of meeting our *human* needs. Rather, this culture is in the business of creating pseudo-needs, even addictions. Therefore it must treat us, and our children, like objects, to be manipulated and fixed. In order for it to thrive, it has to deny our living system status. We become machines without a mind of our own. Our innate intelligence as living beings goes unrecognized, even derided.

One way this is commonly done is by promoting unrealistic, quick problem-solving. Sitcom characters solve dilemmas in less than thirty minutes; commercials imply an end to malaise by purchasing a new car; or the demise of depression with a new color of lipstick; drug companies visually flaunt people we can readily identify with as having more joy in life with the intake of a pill.

Writer H. L. Mencken observed, "For every problem, there is one solution which is simple, neat, and wrong." As humans we know that it often takes more time and energy to solve a problem than we could have imagined. There are always several factors involved. Quick, seemingly easy solutions seldom pay off in the long run. We learn what works by trail and error, carefully weighing choices, and adjusting to outcomes as they present themselves. This takes much effort and on-going determination. The industry-generated culture, however, relies heavily on the mythology that solutions to complex problems come easily. And that mentality has filtered into our way of thinking about what works best for kids. A good example is the prevalence of prescription drugs to counter children's "learning disabilities."

Dr. Lawrence Diller, child psychiatrist and author of several books about the dire consequences of prescription drugs for children, shouts a wake-up call to doctors, parents, teachers, and therapists who are quick to seek a drug to "alleviate a child's suffering." His approach is much akin to treating children as living systems being influenced by their external environment. He points out:

> "[Doctors] confuse symptoms with impairment (how affected are these children really?) and wind up medicalizing what was once extremes of normal coping behavior...People forget that at one time in the 1960s, using the psychiatric standards of the day, sixty per cent of people living in Manhattan were judged to be possibly mentally ill...American psychiatry is missing the big picture...the larger social and cultural factors involved in generating stress and mental illness in kids are ignored...if a child presented with dehydration from acute diarrhea I would treat that child immediately with fluids without waiting to discover the specific cause of the illness. But over time, as I saw more children with the same condition, and learned they were drinking river water possibly contaminated by a factory upstream, it would be unconscionable for me to simply treat the diarrhea without at least raising questions about the source of this contamination."[44]

Mechanistic viewpoints affect parenting profoundly. They keep society's focus on the need for parents to adapt to the craziness "out there," rather than asking, "How can society change to optimally support the real human needs of parents and children?" This considerable parenting challenge brings up the importance of addressing another vital question: How can parents meet their children's real human needs and their own human needs in a larger culture that avoids recognition of those needs?

The Emergence of Unsanity

Under duress, living organisms can make poor choices. Consider a rat that is wired with an electrode in its brain that directly stimulates its pleasure center when it pushes a lever. Given a choice between the lever that stimulates its pleasure center and one that gives it nutritious food, the rat will stimulate its own pleasure center until it starves to death.

Is the rat insane? That is, does it have a deranged mind? No. Does it demonstrate sane behavior for a rat? No. *The rat uses a healthy mind to make "unsane" choices based on what's been done to it from without.* In this case, the imposition of an electrode that is used to stimulate its pleasure center changes the rat's innate pursuit of life-sustaining nourishment. We don't blame the rat for the poor choice. Rather, we see the choice as a reflection of how this animal relates to an unnatural imposition. It's normal for the rat to seek pleasure. It's abnormal for it to seek pleasure that is not connected to its environment in a life-affirming way. Not having any way to understand the conditions that have been imposed on it, the rat normalizes the abnormal, to the detriment of its own life.

The parenting challenges rooted in an industry-generated culture stem from unnatural impositions that cause us to lose a clear focus on our real human needs. Like the rat, we can also normalize the abnormal to the detriment of our lives and the lives of our children. Unlike the rat, though, we *can* come to understand the conditions that are being imposed on us and transform them into conditions that work on our behalf.

Key Questions for Parenting in an Industry-Generated Culture

Question #1:
Whose messages do we want to be most influential in shaping the emerging identity of our children—the messages from an industry-generated culture or the messages from parents?

Question #2:
How do we help our children intentionally choose what is in their best interests when the industry-generated culture and social institutions in our communities persist in urging them to make choices not in their best interests?

Question #3:
How do we nurture our children's and teens' healthy autonomy within an industry-driven culture determined to undermine our authority and responsibility?

Question #4:
How do we parents get the relevant information we need to parent well when that information is not easily available through common mass media channels?

Question #5:
How can we stop the escalation of sensational, mindless content by the industry-generated culture if human brains are easily conditioned to seek it?

Question #6:
How can parents meet their children's real human needs and their own human needs in a larger culture that avoids recognition of those needs?

2
Reclaiming Our Parenting Identity

In the social jungle of human existence there is no feeling of being alive without a sense of identity.

Erik Erickson[1]

Unsane choices can occur unconsciously. For instance, after coming home from a busy day, many working parents have few reserves left to play with children or to do something fun together as a family. Ready, pre-packaged entertainment grants quick relief for fatigued parents. The ease of using screen machines to keep hungry, cranky kids out of our hair while we are frazzled seems to offer a parental oasis. But this seeming respite is really an illusion. It's not a renewal from which we can tap into our own wellspring of creative ideas and build a better life for ourselves and for our children. Rather it's an unsane choice that diminishes our humanity and that ultimately makes our parenting work much more difficult.

Often stay-at-home parents find themselves at the hub of the children's activities and the "go-to-person" for all their needs—from transportation to homework and everything in between. With constant "parental doing" it's understandable that "parental being" would take a backseat. Time for reflection, contemplating decisions, or getting in touch with what really matters can get shortchanged. By-passing the human need for reflection is an unsane choice, albeit a common one.

Avoiding unsanity needs to be a top priority for parenting well in a media age. Since unsane decisions ultimately keep us distanced from our own humanity and that of our children, it's important to have an inner barometer to gauge choice-making. That inner barometer can come from having a very clear parenting identity. Knowing who we are as parents can keep us on track and help us, and our children, to thrive within this nutty environment. By a "parenting identity," I mean those *values, priorities, and actions that reflect who you are as a parent.* When we are strong and sure in our own beliefs, we are energized to find new ways to deal with industry-generated dilemmas. Rather than getting bogged down, we can become re-charged and ready to confront, and even transform, those six pesky challenges of parenting in an industry-generated culture I laid out in Chapter One. With a clear parenting identity we can keep a more objective distance from industry-generated manipulations. We look beyond the sham to what's really important to us.

The fundamental satisfaction, though, of maintaining a clear parenting identity is the model it provides for our children. Being content and clear with who we are helps our children consider carefully who they wish to become. A strong sense of self keeps our parental priorities straight, our authority intact, and allows us a sense of creative freedom in our parenting that we can't get from anywhere else. As parent coach Mary Scribner points out, "Parental authority and family empowerment return as parents lovingly reclaim their role influencing the family and the culture."[2]

In this chapter we will explore how a clear parenting identity brings us more energy and aliveness to be more present and available for our children. We will also look at how a more conscious identity can help us strengthen six internal qualities that add to our parenting repertoire. Here you will also find some reflective questions to ponder. Look at this chapter as a luxury time-out for yourself to think through what you really want for yourself and your children. Without self-knowledge and awareness, we move from task to task, hurried and harried. Our presence and availability to our youngsters can become tentative, our connection to a Higher Power, less conscious. The fact that attending to our children is sacred work can be easily forgotten, even if we remind ourselves at church, synagogue, or mosque each week. In living robotically our life force diminishes. Spiritual damage results, not only for ourselves, but for our children as well. To return to center and know ourselves as spiritual people, as well as competent parents, means reclaiming our identity. Consider how Marge did it.

Marge made contact with me while a working mother of a three-year-old daughter, Lily, and a ten-month-old son, Todd. She wanted help with Lily who was expressing her anger through temper tantrums. Lily was also very clingy and Marge hated leaving her at preschool every morning as she went sadly (and guiltily) off to work. Marge knew that Lily "had not been prepared well" for the birth of Todd, and with his arrival, she realized that Lily felt left out. Marge, a busy bank accountant, hadn't played much with Lily during her toddler years. And then Todd came along.

Marge, with little awareness on her part, managed her life through a series of unsane choices. Trapped in a whirlwind of activity, she reacted to the immediate next thing to do. She had put a TV in Lily's bedroom hoping that it would help the little girl fall asleep. In reality, this made Lily feel more alone and contributed to her angry outbursts. But Marge was too preoccupied to connect these dots. Marge took work home because she wanted to make a favorable impression on her new boss. Up to her ears in paperwork in the evening, she felt bad when she couldn't help her husband put the children to bed. Exhausted and not thinking clearly, Marge had lost touch with her parenting priorities.

Marge and I worked together for over a year. The first three months were the hardest as Marge had to take an honest appraisal of her life both as a mother and as a professional out in the world. During this time period Marge became clearer about what was important to her—spending time with her children while they were young. When Marge admitted to herself what mattered most, she made important changes that made big differences. Playing with Lily for at least a half hour a day and taking the TV out of her bedroom helped the little girl feel more secure. This also made Marge feel more connected, not only to Lily, but to her parenting purpose. Deciding to cut back and work only four days a week was a scary decision. But Marge found it extremely valuable. Spending one whole "festive day" with her youngsters weekly actually made Marge more productive at work. Her boss, seeing her more vibrant and confident, gave Marge a promotion and the go-ahead to work from her home as she needed. Marge was thrilled. She told me, "I actually have more responsibilities now than I did when I first called you. But life is easier and I'm enjoying my children. Plus, they are thriving. Once I got clear about what was most important to me, everything started to fall into place."

The unsanity of parenting in an industry-generated culture has ushered in a parental identity crisis of major proportions.

Webster's dictionary defines an identity crisis as, "confusion about one's social role...a state of confusion in a person or organization regarding its nature or direction." The stresses in Marge's life, for instance, had her looking for the quick-fix of the television in her child's bedroom which could only make the situation worse. Introducing television at an early age would begin a domino effect of parenting problems. Affected would be Lily's self-worth, her habits of mind, and school success years into the future. A few unsane choices can certainly unravel parents' lives and play havoc with the lives of their children. Even though an industry-generated culture can distance us from our true nature, we can get clearer on our parenting identity when we take a little time to stop and reflect on what matters most to us.

Dr. Jane Flagello, president of Direction Dynamics, Inc., coaches business and private clients to feel more empowered. She uses a quick, easy exercise to help people get in touch with their true selves. "Hold up your hand. Your fingers represent the various roles that you play...Your palm represents you. It is the inner you...If you hurt one of your fingers, say you break your pinky...The pinky gets a splint and the rest of the roles continue as if nothing really happened. But let's say you bang your palm and hurt the very center of your hand. The entire hand will hurt. You won't be able to make a strong fist. You won't be able to hold items because the palm controls the fingers."[3]

Chauffeur, chef, role-model, teacher, caregiver—parents wear lots of hats—sometimes more than five fingers, using Flagello's analogy. So how would you define your "parenting palm?" What is the core part inside that forms the basis for all the parenting decisions you make and the roles you play? How do you nurture that part so it is reliable and functional, making it possible for you to do all that you do? Connecting to that core part of ourselves can bring new found self-awareness, along with an exhilarating sense of aliveness.

Defining aliveness isn't always easy. But usually we recognize its presence or absence. In describing figure skaters, while commenting at the 2002 Winter Olympics, for instance, Scott Hamilton distinguished between those that were technically good and those that gave a bit more of themselves, whose passion and "inner glow" caused them to stand out from the others. When have you felt fully alive? Perhaps you recently witnessed a spectacular sunset or smiled quietly, deeply moved as you watched your child sleep. Downhill skiing or bungy-jumping can make many feel intensely alive. Aliveness is more than physical thrills, though. Many women I know, when asked when they have felt most alive, will respond, "When I gave birth." Many men will say, "When I was there at my child's birth." Conversely, we can experience acute aliveness being with someone at the moment of death.

These diverse examples of aliveness all have common characteristics: that of a deeply felt connection to life, along with feelings of transcendence—not always easy to accomplish in today's world. Psychotherapist Gerald May, M.D., writes about this challenge in his book, *Will and Spirit*, "As a culture we now have tremendous difficulty viewing ourselves as part of nature and even more trouble seeing ourselves as children of the universe. Often we sense being brothers and sisters to each other only when we can find a common enemy. We have become so addicted to the self-importance of saying no to destructive forces that we often forget the humble, simple hope of saying yes to life."[4] When we do say "Yes" to life, the ordinary daily events can become extraordinary and the mundane charged with deep meaning. We know we are part of a larger picture. Gratitude for all life and compassion for the human species usually accompanies this recognition, often bringing profound spiritual comfort. Feeling interrelated to all aspects of life, we are centered, energized, and purposeful. An industry-generated culture obviously can't support our realization of connectedness to life. It can't maximize our feelings of aliveness. It can't fuel our spiritual life or nourish our parenting identity. But we can.

Love + Intention + Participation = Parenting Aliveness

Most likely you have exchanged vows with a partner or a spouse. Vows are solemn oaths to honor our commitment no matter what. Since a commitment isn't a bargain in the sense that "I do for you when you do for me," vows can be scary. But we make them anyway. With explicit words and often the exchange of rings, we take a leap into an intimate relationship.

Most of us don't make explicit vows to our babies when they're born. But the strong commitment is there, nonetheless. The vows we make as parents to our children are implicit. Without words, but with actions, we vow to take care of our children and provide for them—no matter what. New York University professors Diane Ravitch and Joseph P. Viteritti make an important point, "Parents...are the only individuals in the world who can be expected to put the interests of their children before anything else."[5] Parental love, by its nature, seeks to protect and nurture children. Part of this love is a primitive urge dating back tens of thousands of years and is determined by the needs of our offspring. For instance, the brain of a chimpanzee at birth, our nearest relative, is one half its full adult size. But the brain of a human infant is just one quarter. The chimpanzee is dependent on its mother for six years—the time it takes for the animal's brain to grow and mature. But the human child is dependent on its parents for close to two decades—the time it takes for the human brain to mature.[6] When parents look out for children it's another way of protecting young brains until fully formed.

Healthy humans have an intentional desire to love and protect their young. This intentionality is a function of our "higher brain." Our reptilian brain, discussed in Chapter One, doesn't form convictions or make choices. Intentionality relies upon our higher-level thinking and spirit of generosity. When tired or stressed, most parents manage to still get dinner on the table, help a child with homework, or quiet a crying baby. The more we lack external resources in our lives, the more we need to rely on our internal resources of will and determination. Indeed, we all have been inspired by people who succeeded despite great odds. What was behind their success? No matter how diverse the challenges, most people succeed because of their intention to do so.

Intention drives our will which keeps us going forward, taking the next step, no matter how weary we may be, no matter what setbacks we experience. Consider any component of the natural world—a tree, a mitochondria, our own hearts. They all willingly participate in life. The maple tree outside my living room window, for instance, doesn't announce, "Today I refuse to participate. I will only be a spectator of life. I will not be involved in my own growth." When our hearts refuse to participate, we have left this world. All of nature actively participates. Humans, though, have the capacity to make an intentional choice in the matter of healthy participation. Even if we blank out the world with drugs or some other addiction, we are still participating in life, only in a diminished, unhealthy way.

When we combine love and intention, what follows naturally is participation. Popular author Marianne Williamson has written, "Love…is not a passive but a participatory emotion."[7] Parental love, fueled by good intentions, roots us firmly in our primary role, actively participating in life with our children for their best interests. Making this role a parenting priority holds many blessings. Its gifts are evident in what happened with Marge.

The more she participated in play and conversation with Lily, the better she appreciated her daughter. She got in touch with her feelings of love for Lily. Love acted as an energizing force to help her keep her commitment for daily mother-daughter play experiences. As she spent more time with Lily, Marge got firmer about what mattered to her as a parent. She was able to set boundaries, find time, and make tough decisions. Being more grounded in her parenting identity, she became more hopeful when the delightful gifts of Lily's better behavior and tender interactions with her younger brother emerged. These positive changes demonstrated to Marge she was on the right track. They helped increase her confidence in other difficult situations with her children.

Marge's love, intention, and participation held an additional bonus. She felt more alive. It took a lot less energy to enter Lily's imaginative world than it took to deal with her temper tantrums. And it was much more fun. As Marge spent more time in play with Lily she found herself getting in touch with the playful, youthful part inside herself. Her increasing feelings of aliveness as a parent spilled over to all aspects of her life, giving her new vitality, hope, and happiness.

The fundamental gift of reclaiming our parenting identity is increased aliveness. With more energy we can pay attention to our own needs and to those of our children. We are more focused on what we really want, not what the industry-generated culture says we should want. With more vitality we can become more vigilant to protect our kids from any forms of negative influences. When we connect to what matters to us and take the steps to "walk our talk," anything is possible. We know that, and so do our children.

More Gifts from a Parenting Identity

Along with increased aliveness, a clear parenting identity also strengthens inner qualities, namely:
- Constancy and Resolve
- Self-Trust and Confidence
- Non-Conformity and Integrity

Constancy and Resolve

Unwavering identity, with a few exceptions, is an obvious fact in the natural world. That lovely maple tree in my front lawn never becomes an evergreen tree. Unless genetically altered by humans, all elements of nature retain their core identity. This constancy of nature is something to think about. Even when the maple tree's leaves turn yellow, are blown off by gusts of wind, and when bright green buds appear, the tree remains what it is. It keeps its identity through snowstorms, hail, an occasional pruning, and numerous visits by neighborhood dogs.

Mother Nature teaches us that a stable core identity provides constancy when the environment around us may change. Understanding the relationship between a stable identity and an unstable environment is a hot topic in the field of business. In her pioneering book *Leadership and the New Science*, Margaret Wheatley writes, "In organizations, just as with individuals, a clear sense of identity—the lens of values, traditions, history, dreams, experience, competencies. . .is the only route to achieving independence from the environment. When the environment seems to demand a response, there is a means to interpret that demand."[8]

The industry-generated culture demands a response from parents. Frantic searching for the latest fad toy, constant reorganization of schedules to accommodate teens' "necessary" shopping trips, and last-minute acquiescence to children's demands as they wear us down with their nagging, are a few of those demands for a response. We frequently are pressured to make quick choices, often catching us off guard. We are less stable when walking through a toy store with a nagging child than we are when we are snuggling with that same child relaxing and reading a nighttime story. In times when the industry-generated culture seems to be "in our face," it's important to allow ourselves some time to understand what it is we want for our child and how the decision we make will serve his or her best interests. A clear parenting identity slows us down to the speed of life. It keeps us out of accelerated overdrive. With parenting priorities at the forefront we have time to interpret demands from corporate-constructed realities. We can center ourselves in what truly matters to us before making hasty decisions we may soon regret. Free, we make our own choices based on what we think is best for our kids, not as pawns in a corporate chess game. Also, our constancy helps our children feel more secure. Children need parental predictability and models for value-based decision-making in order for them to grow into making wise choices as adults.

In a sense, we humans partner with the environment around us to learn and to grow. Like an adept dance partner, an environment that supports our core values can lead us to moving freely and comfortably, creating beauty and grace, a dynamic, exhilarating life. Much of the industry-generated culture, however, proves an awkward dance partner. With a clear parenting identity we can respond "Yes" when it supports us and "No" when it doesn't. A clear identity keeps daily decisions manageable and more streamlined. Saying "No" can move from being a burden we do reluctantly to a delightful experience of affirming who we are and what's important to us. Grounded in our deep core values, we spend increasingly more time doing what gives us most meaning.

Our kids watch every move we make. Their job, especially in adolescence, is to test the boundaries we set. They put up a fuss. Call us "stupid," "unfair," "weird," "not understanding," and maybe even "uncool." This is to be expected. Such resistance on their part is actually saying to us, "Please help me know what is right. Reassure me so I can realize my own potential to be the very best person I can be." With a reclaimed parenting identity, it doesn't mean that setting limits and having our kids stick to them will be any easier. But what does happen is that we stay constant and resolved over time. And our children eventually get the message. Once they know we cannot be moved from our chosen, value-based position, they will decrease their resisting. They may even stop all together. What our children really want, and certainly need, is for us to make it clear to them what we stand for. Once they learn the expectations, children and parents are then at a different level of engagement. Rather than life together always being a battle ground, there is a connectivity between parent and child that wasn't there before. When we set firm boundaries and strive to be consistent with them, our children learn to respect us. Then they relate to us differently. Without that respect from them, they will have a hard time "listening" to us. And that respect from them is hard to come by if we don't expect that they live within the boundaries we set.

Parental resolve can also help us find better ways to support our youngsters. For instance, with resolve, many parents come up with alternatives to television watching. As one mother put it, "I don't think any of us would be exposing our children to television if it were hard to access. I wouldn't go to the hassle of driving thirty minutes somewhere to let them watch *Sesame Street*." Since TV is so easy to access, it takes a deep resolve to pull out the crayons; or help youngsters discover things to do in their everyday experiences such as drawing on junk mail or making finger puppets. Most of these types of activities means we have to be involved to some degree—at least to get young children started. Resolve helps us be on the lookout for ways to help our children and teens learn independence from the industry-generated culture. In so doing, both we and our children achieve freedom from that culture's negative effects.

Self-Trust and Confidence

There is so much information now available to parents through books and websites. This, of course, can be helpful. But any information we find must be filtered through our own understandings of our child and what we think is best for him or her in any given situation. In parenting there is no "one size fits all." Eventually, we must trust our intuition and choose what advice we will put into action. Our confidence, then, becomes indispensable for productive use of expert knowledge. Karen Bierdeman, a mother, teacher, and parent coach, illustrates what commonly happens when we are separated from our own parenting voice: "I am realizing that, as a parent, I am constantly bombarded by the media, just as my children are! Everywhere I turn I see magazines, books and TV shows telling me the 'best' ways to raise my children. Problem is I often doubt myself and sometimes listen; yet, these 'experts' are not in tune with *my* children, *my* values and temperament, nor the temperaments of my children…it's not always easy to hear my own parenting voice amidst all of the clamoring."[9] Too much information surrounding us can make it seem like we must have the information in order to be good parents and live satisfied, fulfilling lives. But actually what matters so much more than finding the right information is our willingness to grow and create our own answers. Our parenting voice, or inner wisdom, is a key component to that growing. Can you hear it? How? When you hear it, do you listen?

All of us, at one time or another, don't believe in ourselves. When we are "outnumbered" and our view is the least popular, whether within the family, the workplace, or in conversation with friends, we may distrust that inner knowing. When we are stressed and know that acting on what we know will take more out of us than we are prepared to give, or when we have to battle and struggle to get our voice heard, it's tempting to give up. When no one else is thinking the way we are or doing what we think is the most sane thing to do, we question ourselves and dismiss that "inner nagging," telling ourselves that what we are feeling or perceiving is just not so. This is especially true when we go against the "conventional wisdom" of mainstream culture. We make waves. We disturb people because the predominant thought of the industry-generated culture has been internalized by most people. We truly can feel isolated, like an alien when we speak our truth. "Conventional wisdom" has been defined as "enculturated consciousness."[10] What is generated in a mass way is easily received by the masses. The consciousness, therefore, in the masses about what is acceptable is formed by an over-arching culture. The collective mind of the American people understands what is worthwhile mainly from the messages of the industry-generated culture. Put bluntly, a lot of conventional wisdom about raising kids just isn't wise. For instance, a *Seattle Times* editorial writer wrote that her "parents' generation had playpens (to keep children occupied,) and we have videos."[11] Both playpens and videos keep kids out of parents' way. True. But to equate them is unsane. Even restricted in a playpen, a child is still moving about and taking in experiences in a three-dimensional world. In front of a two-dimensional flat surface, i.e., a video, however, the child does not explore, experiment, or engage in the sensory world. Arguing these critically significant distinctions, one might be considered "radical" or "preachy." Since "conventional wisdom" says videos for toddlers are fine, a lot of people believe it, even though it's unsane to do so.

In a culture that puts a premium on living by vicarious experiences, it's not surprising to find many distrust their own personal experiences. Sometimes parents don't take seriously what they see happening with their kids. They can see how their children act out, fight, push, shove, get whinny, and are out of sorts after sitting for hours in front of a screen machine. Even if their children are doing poorly in school, reading less because they watch so much TV, sadly, these parents won't take positive actions to counter the situation. They might say, "It's my spouse who has to have the TV on all the time. What can I do?" or "A little TV is OK, isn't it?" Being in denial about what their personal experience is telling them brings much needless suffering to their children. Yes, it takes courage, often a lot of courage, to make a significant change that will be potentially disruptive for others in the family. But ignoring a reality doesn't make it go away. Eventually, consequences have to be confronted.

We can't hide our lack of trust in ourselves from our children. They see it in the decisions we do or don't make. They hear it in our voices. As Leslie Mayer, a parent coach and educator in Anchorage, Alaska points out, "Effective parenting comes from the power within. . .Imagine a corporate work setting where you work in a middle level position. If an immediate supervisor comes to you and gives you a work assignment with the preface that the higher ups want it done this way and you need to do it just so, how would you react? I can see doing the task half heartedly and cutting corners if you can without getting caught. Imagine how your child reacts when you make a request of her without conviction or your authentic power behind it, then the request is paired with a threat if she is noncompliant. If a supervisor came to assign you a task and believed in the value of that task, displayed his enthusiasm for the task, and how he felt you could do a particularly good job at it, would you respond differently? Would your children respond differently if you requested of them in the same manner?"[12]

As we courageously act from our "own parenting voice" and our "authentic power" we demonstrate appropriate authority in relationship to our children. Listening more to our innate wisdom than to media hype, we find an internal strength we didn't know we had. We come to trust our judgments better. It gets easier (although never easy) to say "No," to our kids and mean it. When we operate from our chosen values, in a relationship built on close bonds, we can act confidently to give our children what they need.

Non-Conformity and Integrity

Deb, a grocery store cashier, is an exceptionally outgoing young woman with a quirky sense of humor. She makes customers smile just by being herself. Always coming up with unique ways of self-expression, a lot of people just don't know how to react to her. Once, she intentionally left a substance on her hair for three and half hours in order to strip all of its lush, brown color. Those of us who put substances on our hair to cover-up the gray might find her behavior puzzling. But Deb, as the saying goes, is an original. She can't easily be pigeon-holed. In querying Deb, I found out that she had a life full of varied experiences as a child growing up in South Africa and living in other countries by the time she was eighteen. She exudes confidence and obviously loves being herself.

Deb isn't afraid to stand out or to go against what other people might be doing or not doing. Encountering such people can be rare as there seems to be fewer and fewer folks who "dare to be different." One of the wonderful gifts of reclaiming our parenting identity is that we care less and less "what other people think, say, or do." A non-conformist sees life differently from everybody else. When Quentin Tarantino, director of the ultra-violent movie *Kill Bill* said that "cool parents" would take their children to the movie, a non-conformist might respond, "The guy's nuts to say such a thing." And not be prompted to "cave in" to the pressures from the kids that Tarantino's comment was constructed to initiate.

Non-conformists are traditionally leaders in their fields. Pablo Picasso, George Balanchine, Margot Fonteyn, Freida Kalho, Gandhi—these are just a few cutting edge individuals who "went against the grain" and set new standards in art, science, and social justice in the process. As parents we might not think of ourselves as an artist or a leader in any particular field. But actually we are the core leaders for social transformation. Without us raising kids well, society suffers. Indeed, we not only birth the leaders of the future, we determine to a large degree what that future will look like.

Being different from other parents at your child's school, for instance, may be very difficult—for both you and your child. But if your parenting identity tells you that it's necessary to not conform to the industry-generated influences going on there, your staying true to yourself is actually a leadership choice.

Janet offers all of us a courageous model. She is a mother who makes sure her ten year-old son takes nutritious lunches to school. If we lived in another society, this might not take courage to keep doing such a sane and simple act day after day. But as it is, it takes parental bravery just to keep our kids eating healthily. Janet's son unwraps sandwiches of organic cheeses and feasts on brown rice dishes while his peers eat the more traditional Lunchables™ or similar fare. At times it's hard for him to take the stinging comments from his schoolmates. One day he told his mother, "You know what? If everybody was like our family, then they would be the weird ones, and not me." Janet aches for her son's situation, but was proud of his comment. It shows that he is gaining insight on what his family values, and is learning to take more in stride his "standing out" in the crowd. Janet and her husband put a lot of time and effort into talking with their son about the choices they make and why they make them. They also work hard to have friends in their community who share their priorities, giving their son a chance to interact with these families and their children as much as possible. By being non-conformists we provide a model for other parents and set a new standard as well. Our kids are bound to notice.

But living in our integrity isn't easy. We all experience falling out of integrity from time to time. It's a form of self-hypocrisy that plagues us as humans. As we know somewhere inside us that we didn't follow what we believed in, we can be hard on ourselves. Robert Quinn tackles this side of human nature in his powerful book *Change the World: How Ordinary People Can Accomplish Extraordinary Results*. Quinn reminds us that we cannot escape the consequences of our "integrity gaps." "When we feel ashamed of something we've done," he writes, "we get more divided. We feel bad, in part, because we know that we have the potential to be more than we are, yet here we are choosing to behave in ways that increasingly diminish the self. The more divided we become, the more disempowered, worthless, and unlovable we feel. The divided self is the diminished self, the self in the process of deterioration and slow death."[13]

Our sense of aliveness, along with our wholeness, increases as we stay in our integrity. Quinn explains it this way: "When I clarify my deepest values, my being state tends to change. When my being state changes, I tend to interpret the world differently and I tend to act in more healthy ways for me and for others."[14] Attaining impeccable integrity may be the project of a lifetime. It's an ideal we all strive toward. One thing is for sure: an industry-generated culture gives us many opportunities to practice staying in our integrity.

The following pages provide a few ideas that may be useful.

Ideas for "Walking Your Talk"

Make a regular time to explore the dilemma with someone you respect.

Set aside some time each week, such as a half-hour on a Sunday afternoon when you and your spouse or a caring friend can discuss parenting dilemmas that might push you to make decisions out of your integrity. During the conversation the challenge or challenges are laid out and possible alternatives are discussed. Talk through the situation. For instance, if you are not sure you want your child to go to a certain movie, but your child is being pressured to go by his/her friends, some questions you might discuss are: Do I need to see the movie before I make a decision? Can I read any reliable reviews of the movie? How should I approach discussing this with my child? Are there other movies I can recommend? Would my child consider having the friends come over to our house for a pizza/slumber party and alternative video, instead? What are some creative ways to approach the situation?

Reward yourself for staying in your integrity.

Dr. Diane Dreher, author of *The Tao of Personal Leadership*, gives herself points when she follows her inner guidance. She makes a fun game out of amassing "Conscious Choice in Integrity Learning Points." "I'm such a competitive person," she explains. "I love to give myself points. And besides, no one gives us points for doing things that are good for us. So we need to!"[15] You may also want to consider giving yourself a treat like a massage, an afternoon off to browse a bookstore, or an evening out with your spouse. By consciously celebrating our non-conformity, we build our self-respect and begin to appreciate our power as parents.

Use a journal to "talk through" difficulties you may be facing.

Writing free-flow for fifteen or twenty minutes on a regular basis can be very helpful for expressing strong emotions and putting a situation in perspective. Often a creative idea comes "out of the blue" just by putting down the dilemma on paper.

Go away some place to reflect.

This doesn't mean you have to take an expensive trip to some island. A walk through a local park can give you a half-hour to ponder the situation or dropping the kids off at a friend's house for the afternoon to give you quiet time at home are do-able ways to create some space for yourself. Often with a little solitude comes an exciting solution.

Be mindful of what bugs you.

Pay attention to any inner nagging questions or concerns you have. Take time to sit quietly with the situation and see if the problem is occurring because you may somehow be out of your integrity. You may not have much control over the problem. But use the control you do have to determine if you are in complete harmony with your own truth.

Practice observing the consequences of your choices.

You may find it hard to say, "No," to your child, but when you do, observe the long-term effects on your child when you stay true to yourself in dealing with an industry-generated challenge.

Introducing the Vital Five

With a clear parenting identity we are much better equipped to meet our children's needs. Linda Babin, a school counselor and parent coach, invites the parents she works with to think of themselves as "Master Gardeners" rather than Rembrandts. "The master gardener image suggests that there is already a distinct set of qualities within the child, just like when you plant a tulip bulb in the ground." Linda explains, "When we get confused about how much we can hope to control and shape the beings of our children, we are tempted to think of them more like a blank piece of paper or a canvas upon which we hope to create a beautiful image (typically our image) of what they might ultimately look like or be like."[15]

But children are not blank sheets of paper on which we write. Rather they are Nature's works of art. They have needs to be met. When those needs are met, they grow and thrive just like a healthy garden when it receives what it needs. Parents are not so much in control of how children turn out, as they are in control of the environment in which children grow. As "Master Gardeners" parents provide all the components for children to flourish.

Just as children have essential needs, so do parents. There are five basic, essential needs of all humans that if not met, keep us from blossoming into the rich, full individuals we are meant to be. These needs can easily be thwarted in an industry-generated culture. But they are so vital. Without them we wither, dry up and lose joy and fulfillment. We are more prone to disease because we are not at ease with life. We work against the living system we are in, instead of in cooperation with it. These essential needs not only make us human, they keep us human.

In the next five chapters we will examine these core needs in depth. We will explore how a focus on fulfilling them can get lost in an industry-generated culture, and look at ways to address them pro-actively for increased aliveness—both for our children and for ourselves.

The Vital Five

- A loving parent-child bond

- A rich inner life

- The capacity for image-making

- The ability for creative expression

- Participating as a contributor

Parenting from a Clear Identity

The eight key ideas discussed in this chapter can act as a guide to keep you focused on what works best to parent from a clear identity.

1. Participate in life with your child.

2. Keep in touch with your deep parental love.

3. Strive to remain centered and consistent, especially when under stress.

4. Affirm your parental right to set firm boundaries.

5. Trust your deep knowing. Act with confidence!

6. Dare to be different. Embrace non-conformity.

7. Take time to clarify your values and make conscious decisions based on your integrity.

8. Focus on the five essential human needs each day—for your children and for yourself.

Reclaiming Your Parenting Identity

It may be helpful to reflect upon these questions in order to gain perspective on how your parenting identity may be currently challenged and what you can do to reclaim it.

- How does the industry-generated culture impact the daily decisions you make on behalf of yourself and your children? Do you find yourself "giving in" to your children's whining or to their peer pressure more than you want to? If so, what do you need to do to be better able to "walk your talk?"

- Are you exhausted with trying to respond to the demands placed upon you by the industry-generated culture? Have you discussed this with your spouse, your children? Would expressing your authentic feelings help your family understand your frustrations better? What could you gain by such conversations?

- What brings the most aliveness to you? To your family? How can you do more of these activities without adding stress to you and your children's schedules?

- Who are your best supporters? What family members, friends, or colleagues can you share your frustrations and triumphs with? How can they help you with tough parental decisions?

- What is one step you can take today to get clearer on your parenting priorities and values?

- What courageous action will you commit to that you know to be in the best interests of your child/children?

3

The First Essential Need:
A Loving Parent-Child Bond

Love makes us who we are and who we can become.

Thomas Lewis[1]

The door to the apartment was left ajar, so Miriam peeked in. She knew she was expected, but after knocking several times, she wondered why no one answered. Miriam could see that the blinds were down, making the small room oddly dark for the middle of a rare Northwest sunny afternoon. She called out, "Cindy, Cindy, it's me." But no answer. As Miriam's eyes adjusted to the dim light, she could see Cindy staring at a large television. Cindy's two year-old daughter was enraptured by a cartoon blaring from another TV in the corner of the room. Cindy's son, ten months old, strapped into a car seat, watched a third small television. All three TVs were on different channels.

This true story was told to me at one of my workshops by a public health nurse. At the time Cindy was a sixteen year-old single mother. Understanding the tragedy of this situation, the workshop participants and I discussed how children growing up in a media age who don't get their needs met become parents who can't meet their children's needs. They often use the media as a "parent substitute."

When her daughter Rebecca was born, Cindy was fourteen. Cindy was not comfortable holding, cuddling, or soothing the child. Cindy couldn't find delight in "falling in love" with her baby. It never occurred to her that she would find joy in holding her infant close or speaking and singing to her while looking in her eyes and smiling. Since Cindy didn't have any relatives or extended family, she relied on screen machines to help her parent. When Rebecca cried, rather than holding and rocking her, Cindy put her in front of the TV, leaving her there to "cry it out," sometimes for hours. Neither Rebecca's extreme discomfort nor boisterous rage moved Cindy to respond to her in any way. Often the infant cried until falling asleep, without any physical contact from her mother. When she woke up, Cindy would bottle feed her awkwardly and quickly put her back in front of the TV. When Cindy's son was born, she did the same things with him. Putting the children in front of televisions became daily and nightly routines until health professionals intervened. Yet, with limited parenting skills and lack of understanding about the vital need to interact and bond with her children, Cindy was doing the best she knew how to do.

The startling ease of using screen machines to keep children quiet, yet distant from us, makes emotional bonding a critical parental priority today. Many homes today are often more high-tech than high-touch. With three televisions in the average household, one computer, along with video game systems and hand-held video games, living spaces resemble hectic high-tech offices, instead of comforting, personal havens. Where in the home is the furniture arranged so that family members can face each other and leisurely talk about their day? Does the television on as "background noise" steer family conversations away from personally relevant topics and toward irrelevant industry agendas? Indeed, how do parents and children even find the time and space necessary to converse amid the continual clatter from screen machines? Conversation in the home diminishes with every TV brought into it.[2] Dr. Thomas Lickona, an outspoken and much-needed voice for character education, has found in his research that parents and their elementary school-age children talk with each other an average of ten minutes weekly.[3] He defines "conversations" as more than the parent asking such questions as, "Did you make your bed?" or "Did you do your homework?" Rather, a conversation is a meaningful exchange between parent and child that allows the child to express him or herself and serves as a human vehicle for imparting values. Studies at the University of Victoria put parent-child conversation time at three minutes a day, or less.[4]

Soothing, cuddling, and talking are a few ways human parents respond to their children's cues to develop deep emotional relationships with them. In this chapter, we will discuss the importance of parent-child bonding during infancy and early childhood, and parent-child relatedness during the elementary-school years and adolescence. We will examine the impact of bonding on brain growth, as well as comment on your need to bond with your child to feel happy and satisfied as a parent.

Bonding in Infancy and Early Childhood

Bonding is the first of the Vital Five because without a secure emotional attachment to a parent or caregiver, other human needs can't easily be met. A loving parent-child bond is absolutely imperative to steer brain development on its right course. Love actually changes the shape and function of the human brain. Without such a bond, the child is set up early on for a wide array of future cognitive, emotional, and social problems. In fact, without nurturance from a parent while young, most mammals grow up altered in some way. Rhesus monkeys deprived of mother love, for example, enter adult life with their social capacities permanently damaged and as parents treat their young without affection, like inanimate objects.[5] In other studies, pioneering primatologist Harry Harlow revealed how baby monkeys brought up without mothers and playmates sat in their cages alone whimpering and picking at their skin until they bled, rather than choosing to be with others of their kind, too emotionally damaged to socialize.[6] This is also true of human infants. The nature of the baby's attachment to his or her parent or primary caregiver will be a primary determinant in the child's ability to relate to others. Writing about how the infant internalizes his/her "working model" of how to be with other people from the initial relationship with the primary parent, psychiatrist Daniel Siegel emphasizes: "If this model (the first relationship to the parent) represents security, the baby will be able to explore the world and to separate and mature in a healthy way. If the attachment relationship is problematic, the internal working model of attachment will not give the infant a sense of a secure base and the development of normal behaviors (such as play, exploration, and social interactions) will be impaired."[7]

Young mammals are programmed to attach to what is most present and available in their lives. John Bowlby, British psychoanalyst and psychiatrist, in his classic studies found that baby monkeys will attach to objects. Infant monkeys who were given a "substitute mother" in the form of a cloth monkey clung to it and tried to receive nurturance from it. Separated from their real mothers, they actively "attached" to the only "mother" they knew, even if an inanimate object. Human babies and young children likewise intentionally seek love, comfort, and nurturance from objects. Studies of children who have been separated from their mothers for extended periods of time show a sequence of behaviors that end in detachment from humans and attachment to things. With their mothers unavailable for nurturance, they experienced surprise, then protest, and finally despair. Not understanding that their mothers would come back, these children despaired profoundly. They attached emotionally to a toy or a doll, focusing attention on the object as a source of emotional comfort. As adults many of these children exhibited severe maladjustment, such as high levels of anxiety and aggressiveness.[8]

Even when young children are not separated from their parents, they usually find comfort from inanimate objects, especially when under stress. We only have to think of the importance of a teddy bear or a cozy blanket in our children's lives to know how precious these objects become. Youngsters' propensity to actively seek emotional comfort, even with objects, should give us pause when thinking about putting infants and young children in front of televisions. Programmed by nature to attach and bond with what is present and available to them, do we want our youngsters relying on television programs for solace? Do we want a child by age two to seek and find "nurturance" from a machine? Hardly. Yet, indiscriminate use of small screens with little beings can pave the way for such a distorted, bonded "relationship." The main reason I give when parents ask me about introducing computers in early childhood is that young ones will learn early on to experience the computer as benign. Setting boundaries later for appropriate surfing sites, for instance, can become problematic if the child has formed an emotional attachment to his or her computer. A 2000 study showed that both adults and children increasingly are bonding with their computers as if the devices had a personality. About 40 percent of respondents said they felt "extremely fond" of their equipment, using words that described strong feelings, as if the computer were a beloved friend.[9]

In an age of screens, perhaps one of the basic problems is that it becomes easier for humans to look away from each other rather than toward each other. But humans need to look at each other. Newborns to four-months-olds would rather look at faces than at almost anything else. Rensselaer Polytechnic's Linda Caporael points out what she refers to as "micro-coordination," in which a baby imitates its mother's facial expression, and the mother, in turn, imitates the baby's.[10] This also happens when fathers are interacting with infants. Televisions and computer screens obviously can't accomplish such a profound, coordinated communication. In a sense, children don't know their feelings until the parent expresses feelings for them. Demonstrating a facial expression makes way for the child to understand various emotions and eventually allows for naming those emotions.

Human faces are carefully constructed to communicate emotions. The human face contains more muscles close to the skin than any other part of the body. The authors of *A General Theory of Love* reveal that "...facial expressions are identical all over the globe, in every culture and every human being studied. No society exists wherein people express anger with the corners of the mouth going up, and no person has every lived who slits his eyes when surprised. An angry person appears angry to everyone worldwide, and likewise a happy person, and a disgusted one."[11]

Facial expressions act as a pathway into understanding the other person's inner state. When we think about it, this is an amazing capacity of the mammalian brain. We can't read a goldfish's mood or a turtle's state of mind by looking at. But we can read our pet dog's countenance when we take him for a walk. Mammals use their faces to express emotions. Turning toward each other, parents and young children form a very special interpersonal relationship merely by looking at each other. Since this exchange allows the parent to tune into the mental and emotional states of the child, the relationship bond deepens between them. When we look into the eyes of a beloved person, there is an intimate knowing. When we find vacuity behind human eyes, it can give us chills or cause us to wonder, "What's wrong with that person?"

As parents maintain eye contact with babies and young children it allows these new brains to develop appropriate ways to filter emotional experiences. Watching strangers' faces on flat screens, however, doesn't have the same type of effect for the child. Love must be present and felt for brain structures to respond appropriately.

One of the brain features that distinguishes mammals from reptiles is the limbic brain—the part of the brain that allows us to experience emotions, such as love. The limbic brain works hard to keep us in tune with others' reactions and to keep us engaged appropriately in the world. It's constantly taking in sensory information, filtering it for emotional relevance, and sending outputs to other areas of the brain thousands of times a day.[12] In infancy and early childhood the limbic system develops a boiler plate of acceptable responses based on genetic information and social experiences. When parents nurture, comfort, and talk with infants and young children, they are actually facilitating limbic development. Reptile parents are detached and uninvolved in the lives of their offspring. But mammals interact with their youngsters. As psychiatrist Thomas Lewis reminds us, "The lack of an attuned mother is a nonevent for a reptile and a shattering injury to the complex and fragile limbic brain of a mammal."[13]

Children learn to empathize with others when they feel understood and loved in infancy and early childhood. Limbic health means the child becomes capable of being in healthy, intimate relationships as an adult. Continual, mutually responsive interactions with parents, particularly mothers, set up attunement. And this begins very early. The fetus, for instance, attunes to the mother's voice. Even though the fetus does not have self-awareness, yet, it will display evidence that it knows and seeks its mother's voice.[14] Other examples of attunement can be found throughout the natural world. Scientist Harold Bloom describes a few of them: "Put cells from the eye and the liver in water. The liver cells will gang up with other liver cells; the eye cells will chill with others from the eye...In the growing brain of an embryo, neurons reach for partners with whom they'll spend a lifetime of embrace...And so it goes up the bio-chain...Chimp mothers raising youngsters clot with other toddler-moms, and adult males hang out with other adult males...Sapient humans also follow this primal rule. A Detroit survey of 1,013 men showed that whites tend to choose whites as best friends, Protestants to choose Protestants, Catholics to choose Catholics, Republicans to choose Republicans, and working class to choose working class. Individuals...are pulled together by two kinds of similarity—their emotional wiring and...the extent to which they see things eye to eye."[15]

Brain researchers are now uncovering the fact that in a bonded, emotional loving relationship a phenomena exists called "limbic resonance." This is a special attunement between two or more people which brings comfort and shared meaning. Their limbic brains, or emotional centers, harmonize. Limbic resonance, for instance, takes place when two lovers cuddle. It's not about sex; it's about being in each other's arms and breathing in sync with each other. Before long there is a relaxation response and both bodies begin to regulate in accord with each other. As the emotional centers of both brains resonate, each person experiences a meaningful relatedness.

Similarly holding and lovingly touching our babies brings about limbic resonance and spurs important brain growth. At birth, a baby's brain hold millions of unconnected brain cells. Human touch is absolutely necessary to help these cells connect. Studies have shown that orphans deprived of human touch a few days after birth have seriously altered brains by eighteen months. Their neocortex, or thinking function of the brain, is less developed and less used. Most of their brain activity takes place in the reptilian system, causing the children to be hyperactive and aggressive, with serious attention problems.[16]

To summarize the crtical importance of limbic resonance, let's return to the writers of *A General Theory of Love:*

> "Only through limbic resonance with another can [the child] begin to apprehend his inner world. The first few years of resonance prepare [the child's brain] for a lifetime's use. One of a parent's most important jobs is to remain in tune with her child, because she will focus the eyes he turns toward the inner and outer worlds. He faithfully receives whatever deficiencies her own vision contains. A parent who is a poor resonator cannot impart clarity. Her inexactness smears his developing precision in reading the emotional world. If she does not or cannot teach him, in adulthood he will be unable to sense the inner states of others or himself. Deprived of the limbic compass that orients a person to his internal landscape, he will slip though his life without understanding it."[17]

In addition to supporting the child's emotional and social development, early bonding experiences also help grow smarter brains. Sometimes we separate the brain into two compartments: feeling and thinking. But this is more for our convenience of categorizing and talking about its different functions. In reality, emotional and intellectual structures are interwoven. Help one and you help the other. For instance, as we sit comfortably reading to our youngsters, we know it will support their literacy and school success. But at the same time, limbic resonance works its magic, too. The closeness of a loving parent nurtures the child's emotional well being, calms any stress the child might be experiencing, and generally acts as a healing event for both parent and child.

How does cuddling, talking, singing, and laughing with youngsters help their intellect? Well, for critical thinking skills, a brain must be well-organized. In addition, it needs to be coherent, with various parts working in harmony with each other, like a happy family. Exciting new brain research reveals that emotional bonding in the early years with a parent helps the thinking part of the brain organize and harmonize in four specific ways.

First, during nurturing encounters with a parent, the child's brain starts learning what to value. In fact, brain researchers have found that "emotion is fundamentally linked to the same circuitry that is responsible for creating meaning and value..."[18] In other words, if we want our children to grow up valuing learning, for instance, link learning to emotional bonding experiences early on. If we desire our child to value him or her self, give plenty of loving affirmations while the child is young.

Second, during interactions with caring adults, the child stores away those experiences in memory and uses them later to make choices. Young brains learn about their world by creating inner pictures, or mental models. For example, if infants are allowed to feel the shape of a nipple with their mouths in a darkened room, they later will be able to pick out the familiar nipple from a visual display. Their minds have created a mental image from touch which can then be used to sense a familiar pattern by sight.[19] The baby and the young child need lots of loving encounters through their senses. These, in turn, help the child create generalizations from experiences. They set the stage for the child to be able to have problem-solving skills later.

Third, healthy attachment in the early years helps the child regulate strong emotions in order to be able to learn. A loving bond with parents as an infant enables a child to later persevere through difficult learning experiences without getting overly frustrated or angry. Secure children are much more likely to be in control of their emotions and to talk themselves through a challenging task instead of letting anger or frustration take over. The first step in learning patience is having a brain that can regulate emotions.

Finally, the parent-child bond supports cognitive development through mutual engagement in the sensory world. As parent and child play together, the sensory world pours into the child's nervous system. Movement and tactile experiences actually trigger neural networking. That is, actual brain structures, particularly the synapses that allow for communication among brain cells, are determined by a child's physical exploration of the world. These structures cannot grow any other way. There's a big difference between drawing with a mechanical device to "form" lines on a computer screen and drawing by immersing little hands in watercolor paint, forming lines on textured paper. The smell and feel of the paint, the experience of making the lines by allocating the paint, the touch of the paper—all combine to activate brain circuitry in ways that cannot be done in front of flat sterile, screen surfaces. Direct experience with the concrete world is imperative to grow the young human brain. With an estimated one quadrillion potential nerve connections in the brain, at any one time the possible combination of messages jumping across the synapses exceeds the number of atoms in the known universe.[20] That's the vast human potential. The more parents lovingly interact with young children and model active participation in the natural world, the greater the chances that the youngster will develop more of his or her capacity. Just doing simple activities like taking a walk together sets up limbic resonance, shared communication, direct experiences, and important bodily movement. We shouldn't underestimate what a "little thing" like taking a walk with a child can do for his or her "brain gain." A summary of over eighty studies link movement with memory, spatial perception, language, attention, emotion, nonverbal awareness, and decision-making.[21]

Dr. Craig Ramey of the University of Alabama found in various studies spanning thirty years of research that he could increase connections between brain cells of infants and young children by increasing their interactions with their environments. Children who were exposed daily to age-appropriate toys, interaction with friends and adults, and activities which prompted self-directed exploration, and who were given the proper nutrition, were found to have higher intelligence quotients than a control group of children with a similar background. In at least eleven separate studies, Ramey found data to show that if interventions to provide a cognitively rich environment did not occur before twenty-four months, the children would be seriously delayed. In an interview he has stated: "The quality of the environment and the kind of experiences children have may affect brain structure and function so profoundly that they may not be correctable after age five. If we had a comparable level of knowledge with respect to a particular form of cancer or hypertension or some other illness that affected adults, you can be sure we would be in action with great vigor."[22]

When infants have the appropriately enriched environments, the chances are far greater that as young children their brain will grow properly. The recognition that stimulation is crucial to development, however, has led to misguided attempts to create superbabies with all types of extraneous toys, regimes, even videos. Anneliese Korner, a professor of psychiatry and premature infant research at Stanford University School of Medicine emphasizes the importance of the bonding experience over any particular methods. "The mother herself is such a rich sensory stimulus that a baby doesn't need a lot of equipment. These gadgets parents buy with the idea that they can accelerate development or substitute for the mother's time are ineffective, and the over stimulation they can supply can be a problem."[23] There is no replacement for a loving parent-child bond.

Ideas for Bonding with Your Baby

You won't smother your baby if you sleep with him or her. A baby's physiology is really unprepared to sleep alone, isolated from parents. If you are wary of having your baby in bed, then keep your baby in your room. But seriously consider the following research from Dr. James McKenna, a world expert on sudden infant death syndrome: McKenna videotaped segments of mothers and infants sleeping together that showed when the mother moves in her sleep, the baby also moves, their patterns remaining reciprocal even while asleep. Robin Karr-Morse and Meredith Wiley, writing about Mc Kenna's research note that mother and child form a communication bond, even in sleep. "Movements and sounds by one generate movements and sounds by the other. These sequential exchanges, he [Mc Kenna] says, account for the maintenance of the baby in relatively lighter states of sleep that prevent the infant's descent into what he calls stage-five sleep, which can lead to lethal SIDS [Sudden Infant Death Syndrome.]"[24]

Stay close to your baby during the day

- As you walk around doing light chores, use a snuggly so your baby can be close to your body and feel your heartbeat.
- Sing quiet songs or hum restful melodies as you rock your baby slowly in rhythm.
- Make as much eye contact as you can with your child by playing facial games of imitating various expressions, talking with your child, singing, cooing and basically having as much fun interacting with your baby as you can. Delight in her every new achievement; affirm every time he tries something new.
- Take care of yourself. You can only interact with and enjoy your baby to the degree that you have the energy to do so. Asking for help and accepting support for household tasks and other duties that require your attention means that you have more attention for your child. You will not regret the time and love you lavish on your baby. A secure infant is on a trajectory for a fulfilling life.

Ideas for Bonding with Young Children

Toddlers, preschoolers, and kindergarteners are very busy and so are we! Here are some ideas for bonding with them throughout a busy day:

- Take twenty minutes in the morning and twenty minutes in the evening to play with your child. Make a room out of a blanket over the kitchen table or build a tower with blocks with your child, you will learn much about how your child perceives his/her world. You also strengthen your child's feelings of security, trust, and belonging.

- When in the car running errands, point out what you see and discuss various colors and shapes. Talk about what you will be doing, such as: "First we're going to the Post Office. Then we'll go grocery shopping." Give your child something age-appropriate to do, such as dropping a letter into a slot at the Post Office or choosing apples to put in the cart at the grocery store. Affirm all efforts. Keep your child involved in the process.

- Slow down the pace of your day by talking with your child. A conversation interlude with a little one can be very poetic and awe-inspiring. Often youngsters say and see things from an interesting and unique perspective. Their self-expression blossoms with parental attention and authentic curiosity. Some questions you may want to ask: How would you describe_____? What else could _____ be? If you could change _____ what would you do?

- Have other adults to talk with. Especially if you are a stay-at-home-parent or a single parent, make it a priority to have a weekly conversation or get-together with a trusted friend. You will be much more present and available to your child when you have predictable breaks for adult conversations away from your child.

Bonding with Children, Ages 6-10

Babies and young children deliberately bond with us, continually seeking love and comfort. As our children grow into middle childhood and begin their journey toward independence, it is we who have to become more intentional about keeping and deepening the parent-child bond. Because this stage of development warrants exploration of children's skills and talents, it's tempting to keep them very busy with music or dance lessons, sports, and other extra-curricular activities. But really what matters most is the time we spend relating to them.

There's been a lot of talk and controversy over parent-child quality time. Have you ever defined what "quality time" with your child or children would mean? What does it look like? Do you know when you experience it? Does your child? Reflecting on what makes quality time *of quality* can be interesting and can help busy parents orchestrate the types of experiences they want with their children. For quality time to strengthen the parent-child relationship, it would be characterized by three important elements:

- An experience of shared feelings
- A valuing of each other
- A recognition of connection

Most parents can give examples of times with their children that reflect these three elements. One mother of a nine year-old son told me, "When I take Isaac to soccer practice, he usually tells me about his day. In the car, it's just he and I. We don't even turn the radio on because there is just this great atmosphere of sharing. He'll tell me about his day, the good things, the not-so-good things. I listen as best as I can and ask him questions to find out more how he's thinking. I'm always fascinated by what he says. He has great insights for a kid his age. He'll give me a quick hug before he gets out of the car and look me in the eyes with a sheepish grin. Usually, he says, 'Thanks, mom.' We both know he's thanking me not only for the ride to the soccer field, but for something intangible as well."

This mother obviously values her son, and her son, in his own way, shows he values her. She makes emotional space for him to be able to talk to her by limiting the distractions when they are together in the car. In making the regular drive to soccer practice a reliable opportunity for shared time, she nurtures the connection between them—even in the midst of a busy day. Of course, a lot of times when we're driving our kids to sports' practices or other activities, we have their friends in the car with us and can't use the time for a parent-child sharing. That's understandable. The important thing is that during this stage of our children's development, we use the time we do have to intentionally bond with them.

I was shopping with my husband about a week before Thanksgiving one year and saw something I will never forget. A young girl, around eight years-old, was with her mother. As they traveled down the aisles, the mom had to steer her daughter so she wouldn't walk into anything because the girl's face was buried in a Gameboy. Not talking to each other, mother and daughter walked around the grocery store as if robots being given marching orders by the hand-held device. The only time they looked at each other and spoke was when the Gameboy malfunctioned. They were trying to figure it out in front of the meat counter, as people huddled around them trying to pick up their Thanksgiving turkeys. The two were oblivious to the impatient crowd. The Gameboy held their attention until, finally, it was fixed. Then they continued as before, walking the aisles, mother wordlessly steering daughter, with daughter fixated on the small screen.

For parents, grocery shopping may not be the most exciting event. But with a child before a holiday it can be an opportunity to talk about plans for Thanksgiving dinner; pointing out varieties of brightly-colored gourds, commenting on the beauty of the flowers on display, and discussing buying decisions. If we don't consider such a mundane task as grocery shopping as significant, the industry-generated culture can waltz right in and disrupt the parent-child bond, as in the case between that mother and her daughter. Gameboys are played, not only in grocery stores, but also during family gatherings so kids don't have to listen and respond to relatives' "boring" conversations; during long car trips, so kids will be quiet; and at sporting events so younger brothers and sisters don't have to watch their older siblings make a basket or score a goal. Thinking that such screen machine distractions are benign can be dangerous. Elementary age kids will attach to objects similar to how young children do. Dr. Donald Shifrin, a pediatrician and an active member of the American Academy of Pediatrics cautions parents not to buy any video game system, even Gameboys. "If you watch kids playing these games, you will see a definite drug response. That's way I'm adamant about this issue. Like wearing seatbelts or car helmets, there are no exceptions for me."[25]

We can communicate to our kids that we value them in many ways and places. We will never get the "right time" or the "perfect setting" to strengthen our relationship with them. That means it's wise to think of the times that we do have as very important opportunities to bond with them. Jewish theologian Martin Buber proposed two ways of human interaction. An "I-It" approach where we view the other as an object, distant from us, like a thing, without a soul. Or an "I-Thou" approach where the other is valued as a unique person to be appreciated in his or her own right—a sacred being. I don't think that parents rearing children in an industry-generated culture are conscious of treating their kids like objects. But steering a child around a grocery store as if she were a wind-up doll fits the description. So does silencing children in front of screen machines, for any reason. When kids are treated like objects both by the culture and the family, they can be expected to be enraged. Most can't articulate that rage easily. That's one reason it pours forth in depression, suicide, and escalating levels of violence and brutality as many U. S. children grow older. They might advance in age, but if they see themselves as objects, they won't mature. Healthy emotional well-being depends upon youngsters understanding themselves as important human beings to be cherished. Parents demonstrate that through countless seemingly mundane activities. It's in the simplicity of our lives with our children that they can experience our profound love.

Louise Barbee is an educator and parent coach in Walnut Creek, California. Her own two children are now young adults, so she has the perspective both as a professional well-versed in child development and as a mother who can look back from experience. She points out that often when we are caught up in some struggle with our kids we will see only a part of our son's or daughter's personality. At such times she notes, "Our attention is diverted to see only segments of the child causing us to focus on particles of their being, leaving a whole universe of their self unrecognized."[26] Consciously bringing in the three elements of bonding (sharing, valuing, and connecting) when we interact with our children is a way to pay attention to the "whole universe" of who they are, even during difficult times. In so doing, we approach our children from an "I-Thou" standpoint, which allows for authentic emotional intimacy to emerge. Louise adds some other important considerations: "Much of the work I do with parents is helping them to understand that we teach our children how to treat us. By our actions we elicit certain behavior from our children. We can change the way our children treat us by first changing the way we treat them. While growing up my own children were always telling me that I treated them differently than their friends were treated by their parents. When I asked them in what way, they would respond that I treated them like they were valued members of the family and that their opinions mattered."[27] Parents who treat their children respectfully may be considered "too liberal" or "trying to be their children's friend." Respecting our kids doesn't mean giving up our authority. Rather when we gain our kids' respect, we have appropriate parental authority. They listen to us better because they trust us to act in our integrity on their behalf.

Productive love that can transform another human being has four major qualities: care, responsibility, knowledge, and respect.[28] It's easy to understand the parental role as one of care and responsibility. Likewise, we must be knowledgeable about our children in order to meet their needs. But somehow, the quality of respect isn't naturally ascribed to the parent-child bond. Yet, during the ages of six through ten, if children don't come to respect their parents and vice-versa, adolescence can be more difficult than it has to be.

Without validation human beings despair. We all want to be seen and recognized for who we are. We all need to feel like we belong. Humans long for that. Parental respect validates children and enables them to feel significant. As we spend time with our children we not only silently express that we value them, but we also silently tell them that we value our parental role. Let's face it, when kids are left in an emotional void without parental guidance, what are some conclusions they can easily come to? That they aren't worth the parent's time. And that the parent disdains his or her job because the child is so horrible. In thinking that they aren't good enough, children can easily escalate those thoughts to resent the parent's absence. Yet, understand it, too. "After all, maybe my mom or dad would like being parents better, if I were better," a child might think to herself. As we validate our kids, we also validate ourselves as parents in their eyes.

When we pattern our lives to weave into the daily grind moments of delightful sharing with our youngsters, we positively shape our youngsters' self-identity. Also, we imprint positive messages inside our kids' heads. The parental voice is by its nature, very powerful. The damage negative talk from parents can do is evidenced in the growing counseling and healing industries. But the parental voice can work powerfully for good. Just by being with our kids and making appreciative comments, keeping curious and affirming their ideas and efforts, we make a lasting impression on their future self-talk. As adults, children who have had the advantage of the presence and availability of a loving parent are much more likely to be gentler with themselves and talk to themselves in kind ways when presented with life's many challenges.

During this developmental period, peers start playing an important role. With a strong parent-child bond, children will develop healthy peer relationships and not be unduly influenced by the need to "be like so and so." Some experts believe that parents matter less than peers in terms of long-lasting influence on kids.[29] A thirteen-year longitudinal study, however, by anthropologist Mark Flinn refutes that position. By measuring the stress hormone cortisol in children several times daily for years, Flinn has thousands of data points and one pattern shines through all the others. "Families matter more than anything else in a child's life. When a family has problems, it sends stress hormones coursing through a child's system. When family members get along, or have numerous relatives to call on, they can shelter a child from the worst social upheavals in the outside world. Emotionally and physiologically, family life is ground zero for a child's health."[30] Flinn found that fights or upsets with peers did little or nothing to effect children's stress levels, but a problem in the family? Well, that sent stress upward consistently. Although his study was conducted in a quiet village of Bwa Mawego, in the Caribbean, it has relevance for U.S. parents. There are serious family situations today that create much stress for kids, divorce and domestic violence being perhaps the most obvious. Combine that with our fast-pace of everyday life and the clamoring of visual media. If stress hormones can rise in children living in a slow-paced, less-industrialized culture like Bwa Mawego, how much more can they rise within our society?

Unlike in Bwa Mawego, however, in our culture a break with a friend may prove just as stressful as an argument with a parent. Because children and their peers are living systems within an industry-generated culture, peers take on a unique significance. Here's how:

The human need to belong will not go away and can become re-routed from parent to peer. When children are not in a loving child-parent bond, they will more likely attach to peers. If parents withdraw and don't make their bonding with their children primary, then as children reach the age of eight or nine, they are faced with "an unbearable and unnatural attachment vacuum," according to family physician Dr. Neufeld and therapist Gabor Mate, authors of *Hold on to Your Kids: Why Parents Matter*. To fill that void, kids bond with people their own age and wind up "peer-oriented."[31]

This is an untimely orientation to peers. Children need loving adults to guide them to learn social mores and standards of behaviors. Without time with such adults and with little respect for the adults they do spend time with, children won't be equipped for adulthood. Since they've stopped listening to the adults around them, they have no reference point for what it means to be a human adult. What they do listen to, though, are TV, radio, DVDs, CDs, and video games. The industry-generated culture convinces children that certain toys, or attitudes, or behaviors are needed in order to be "cool" and to fit in with their friends. Of course many children will believe this.

With a weakened child-parent bond, the parent loses authentic authority. The child does not want to spend time with parents and spends more time with peers. The parents are OK with this because they are having a hard time relating to their children anyway. But the parents are not thinking that the peers are merely parrots of the industry-generated culture. The child and his or her peers spend their time talking about and focused on industry-generated ideas. This increases the chances that the parent's control and influence will continue to erode. These industry-generated ideas are familiar to the child, having been with them four or five hours a day since toddlerhood. It's natural for the child to gravitate to peers who talk about and think about like-minded ideas. It's only human to feel safe and find comfort in the known. As parents rail about the "media's influence" and fail to spend time with their children to deepen their bonds they push children into the arms of their peers. Children will always opt for the certainty of knowing who they are and where they belong. Nowadays a lot of them find that with their friends.

This scenario is the ultimate in destroying the parent-child bond. How do we mitigate it or escape its tyranny entirely? We take ourselves seriously as parents and affirm the parent-child bond as imperative. We also reduce children's stress.

The work of child psychiatrist Mary Burke calls critical attention to the alarming rate of children more stressed out than ever before. Burke has documented case studies of high levels of stress and anxiety in children, correlating directly to overexposure to what she terms, VEM, visual electronic media. In many of the instances, the child's attachment with the parent was severely altered. Here is one of her case studies:

> "Ann is a delightful little girl of six, who presented with partial panic attacks when separated from her mother, accompanied by the vivid belief that her parents were dead. She was unable to accept soothing from any other adult. She had no previous psychiatric history...She spent three hours a day watching television/videos and was obsessed with watching *Harry Potter*. A play evaluation quickly revealed her fear of 'bad magic' characters who killed parents and could not be defeated. She was preoccupied with the visual image of Voldemort drinking a unicorn's blood and of Harry Potter's doomed mother's face. After all her scary videos were ceremonially locked away and screen time was sharply reduced (with a concomitant rise in family activities), the symptoms ceased."[32]

If children experience anxiety in the home it stands to reason that they will look outside the home to feel less stressed. When children spend more time with parents in fun activities that allow for sharing of feelings, valuing each other and feeling connected, the parent-child bond grows and develops the resilience needed for the coming teen years.

Ideas for Creating Space for Bonding

A part of our job as a parent in a media age is to be a "space creator." We can limit distractions so that there is space for parent-child sharing. Some ways to allow for meaningful conversations with our children include:

- Keep the TV off when no one is watching.
- Sit down and take ten minutes to be there when you know your child will be in the room. Don't read or do anything. Say you are having some down time, but you can be interrupted.
- Invite your son or daughter to a book talk or lecture at the local library or museum on a topic of mutual interest. Afterwards share your thoughts together over a meal or snack.
- Make it a family ritual that you and your spouse spend one-on-one time with each of the children on a regular basis. Some families find that taking each child out to dinner offers opportunities to ignite conversations that might not take place around the family dinner table.
- Make time on the weekend, such as a Friday evening, a Saturday afternoon, or a Sunday morning that would specifically be set aside for a special activity with your son or daughter—such as a long walk together, working

together on a house project like cleaning out the garage, or discussing and helping with homework. Keep this time sacred and don't allow your child to schedule anything else during it.

Strengthening the Parent-Teen Relationship

A psychiatrist friend of mine told me as my sons and I were navigating adolescence, "If your teens aren't driving you crazy, they're not doing their job." Well, I thought, thank you very much. They are doing a fine job, as half the time I was worried sick and the other half I was arguing with them, over one thing or another. Not real conducive to loving bonding. I found that the turbulent teens were much like the terrible twos, except you could reason better with a two year-old than you could with a fifteen year-old.

In all the hassles that come up between children and parents during adolescence it's important to remember that if we have done our job well, their job will be to break away from us. We can no longer develop our bond and in many ways we must let it go. But as we shall see, we can do things to strengthen the bond, so that after they find themselves as adults, they will come look for us. And being in their early twenties, with a successful adolescence behind them, parent and child can begin the new adventure of learning how to be adults together. That's how it's supposed to work. But what to do in the meantime?

First, it's important to remember that the teen brain is still growing and all the gray matter is not there yet, no matter how sophisticated your teen may want to appear. The human brain reaches full maturity at age twenty-two or twenty-three. So trying to explain something logically to your teen may not always click.

During these years more than fifty percent of neural connections are eliminated.[33] The pruning allows for important functions to take over, and they eventually do. But not until the early twenties. Until then a simple answer you think you're giving can turn into an endless hassle. Keeping our responses short and to the point can help alleviate a potential blow-up. Also using a firm voice with confidence can be very productive as teens will respond to the most expedient. If your voice carries authority, they will catch that quickly.

A second important consideration is that most parents have to work very hard to allow their children to break their bond with us. We naturally want to hold on, especially mothers. So being gentle with ourselves is crucial. Supporting ourselves to support our teens goes a long way to strengthen a roller-coaster relationship.

It helps to use appreciative language as much as we can. Giving teens choices, acknowledging all the skills they do have, and showing them that we value their contributions are worthy parental communication skills. Approaching teens from an appreciative view without being Pollyannish about it, demonstrates to them that we truly care and that no matter what, we are there for them.

Teens need people they can admire. Even if they disagree with us, they won't lose respect for us if we stay true to what we believe is in their best interests. We are their role models and as such, we can introduce them to other adult role models. Diane Dreher has found that "research on today's college students reveals some disheartening statistics: nearly eighty percent of the ninety-four undergraduates I surveyed last year said they had no models or mentors to help them live meaningful lives. For those few with role models, one third of these were limited to sports figures and pop stars. I know that as a young person I benefited tremendously from positive role models. I read Eleanor Roosevelt's autobiography in high school and her influence has been with me ever since. As an undergraduate at UC Riverside, I heard Linus Pauling speak on campus. With a group of students sitting around him on the lawn in the late afternoon sun, he told us about his life's work for science, discovery, and peace. The sun's parting rays were at his back, but he had his own light, positively radiating energy and enthusiasm. Linus Pauling's bright spirit has been a guide for me ever since."[34] It's interesting to note that Diane has focused much of her adult life working for peace. She wrote a highly-acclaimed book call *The Tao of Inner Peace* and she was instrumental in initiating a Peace Studies Program at Santa Clara University. What moves us as young people can have far-reaching consequences. By guiding our kids to learn from inspiring adults we shape their future decisions. As adults, they will remember that and appreciate it. Our relationship with them ultimately benefits.

Another way to nurture relatedness with teens is to tell them stories. We usually think of story-telling as something we do only with little kids. But older kids and teens (as well as adults) like a good story. Perhaps the television and movie habit is nothing but a natural search for story. The human mind was shaped over thousands of years through oral storytelling around a community fire. Today's electronic hearth replaces that vital tradition. C. R. Synder, Diane McDermott, and William Cook writing in their book, *Hope for the Journey*, maintain that "stories are the very stuff for constructing and maintaining a sense of hope in children."[35] Considering that so many of our youth fall into depression during adolescence, stories told by the people who love them can catalyze a renewed sense of optimism. In fact, the most significant way to counter negative, nihilistic mass stories is for parents to tell personal positive stories. Synder, Cook, and McDermott also point out that while listening to stories "the child is creating a storehouse of special talents from within—tales in which the child forges new territory and overcomes obstacles."[36] This can also occur with teens. Youth is a particularly important time for exploring new ideas, along with deepening self-understanding.

Stories will help your teen see a different side of you. They bring you and your teen together over common terrain, and mutual appreciation is often an important by-product. Tell stories about your family's traditions, how they came about. Tell about grandparents' falling in love; give details about their wedding day. Tell stories that inspired you when you were a teen. Collect stories of everyday heroes from the newspaper and share them at the dinner table in an off-hand manner. Buy biographies of accomplished people and give them to your teen as a spontaneous gift. Don't let mainstream media be the primary story-teller in your child's life. You take on that role. Teens are about to launch their adult years. Hopeful stories about real people will teach them how to fly.

Appreciation Strengthens the Parent-Child Bond

The following are examples of statements and questions you can use to express appreciation to your child. They are divided into three categaories: for children ages 6-10, 11-14, and 15-18.

Appreciative statements and questions for children, ages 6-10

- What I most appreciate about the way you handled that situation was...
- I very much want to hear what you have to say, so I'm going to stop cooking dinner for a while and let's sit down and talk this over.
- When we play checkers (chess, board games, etc.) I really enjoy watching you think.
- I so love spending this time with you!
- When we work together in the (garden, kitchen, etc.) I notice that you...and I really appreciate that about you. Do you notice that about yourself, too?
- Did you know your eyes light up and you glow when you are creating something new like...
- I love watching your curiosity (imagination, thinking, kindness) at work.
- You have many talents and skills. Which ones do you like best?
- I admire how you are taking good care of your (dog, kitten, schoolbooks, etc.) You are learning to value what's important.
- I cherish you!

Appreciative statements and questions for children, ages 11-14

- I very much want to hear what you have to say and I want to be able to listen to you. Right now I'm trying to get dinner ready, but I'll stop if you think it's important. Or we can talk after dinner. Your choice.
- Sometimes it takes courage and integrity to be your unique self. What do you appreciate about yourself

for not going along with your friends in this situation?

- I hope you are valuing all the effort you put into...
- I want you to acknowledge yourself for...
- I know you are feeling badly right now and wish your friend was nicer to you. What can you do to be gentle with yourself until you feel better?
- I'm really grateful for all your help (around the house, when I was sick, with our move, etc.). I hope you know how important your contribution was.
- I'm glad that we don't have to agree and that we can still respect each other's opinions.
- I think it's very positive you can express yourself so well. How are these strong feelings serving you right now?
- I can see that you struggled with that choice and I admire that you took the time you did.
- I am so glad you see that family time is just as important as time with your friends.

Appreciative statements and questions for teens, ages 15-18

- Mother to daughter: I know you want to spend Friday night and Saturday at Sally's house and that's fine with me, if we can be sure we will have next weekend for a special time together. What would you like to plan to do?
- Father to son: Spending Saturday hiking with John and his family seems like great fun. Next weekend I'd like you and I to take some time to...
- I am growing to respect the adult in you that I see emerging.
- Sounds like that was a tough decision, but you made it!
- I like what I'm seeing in this report card. Your commitment

to your academic progress will serve you well.

- I admire how you are taking care of your health (responsibilities, college application, etc.)
- I appreciate the seriousness with which you are approaching drivers' education.
- You know how to make good decisions on your own behalf. Would it help if we discussed the pros and the cons before you decided one way or another?
- I can see that you are trying to understand me and I value that greatly. As you get older, sometimes it's hard for me to let go.
- What you have to say is always important to me. And I appreciate you sharing.

Parents are People, Too: Gaining from the Parent-Child Bond

The obvious result for us of a loving bond with our children is continued love and respect from them. But even more than that, we need to bond with them for our own needs, separate from theirs. With a fragile parent-child bond, life is more difficult for parents, too. We move out of the role as parent and into one of a controller or director, ever trying to force, cajole, nag, and persuade our kids to listen, behave, and do "as we say." A loving bond makes it easier for children to obey because they feel loved. Many well-intentioned parents who love their kids deeply have a difficult time conveying that love. The kids just do not feel loved. If the relationship between parent and child is not constructed from a deep foundation of loving interrelatedness, it will be difficult for parents to demonstrate "enough" love so the kids know it is there. The felt experience of love through a strong parent-child bond reassures the child and makes parenting a richly satisfying experience—one more exhilarating than exasperating.

Since we are human, we will make mistakes. No one ever parents perfectly. No one should ever expect to parent perfectly. When we have a strong relationship with our kids, however, the mistakes we make will have less severe consequences. Our kids will be able to make sense out of our failures and forgive us our faults. With a loving bond with our kids, then, we don't so much try to do things, "by the book," but more from a felt need to be loving toward our children. When we make a decision that is off the mark, we can get back to center more quickly because we put our relationship with our kids at front and center. We then experience continual growth of our parenting skills. Love is the ultimate teacher. By letting it guide us, we learn, grow, and develop new ways of understanding our children, as well as ourselves.

Limbic resonance in infancy and early childhood sets up a joyful relationship between parent child. When we have that kind of felt connection with another human being, we both like being with each other. Life together is fun and full of delight. There are so many parents who are sad, troubled, or even heart-broken during their parenting journey because their bonds with their children are frayed. They are weary. Many become bitter. Our natural human right as families, however, is to enjoy each other and experience deep joy in being together. A loving parent-child bond makes that possible as it energizes us—as people and as parents. Maybe it's not a coincidence that the word, "bond," rhymes with "fond." The bonds we develop and maintain with our children surround us with an enlivening love. Each day with our child, then, becomes a treasured time; an awesome adventure—just the way it was meant to be.

To Strengthen the Bond with Your Children

Each of us as unique parents will find different methods for developing bonds with our kids. If any of the ideas mentioned below work for you, then those are what you want to pay attention to and make an important part of your family's daily life.

- I find that the better I take care of myself, the more present and available I am to my children. So I make sure I invest time in my own health and well-being.

- I make sure I do something each day with my child that excites and energizes us both.

- I set aside three or four regular intervals each day to talk with my child.

- When I find my mind wandering when my child is talking to me, I admit it, suggest we talk another time, or I gently bring myself back to the present moment.

- I consider how my parents developed a loving bond with me (or a not-so-loving bond with me) and I learn how to be a better parent from my own childhood experiences.

- I ask for feedback from spouse and friends on ways I can more lovingly and consciously bond with my child.

- I ask my child what works for him or her to have enjoyable time together.

- I look for ways to keep distractions to a minimum so my child feels free to open up to me.

4

The Second Essential Need:
An Interior Life

*We need a massive investment of talent and discipline
in our inner lives.*

Matthew Fox[1]

Greg, an accomplished geologist and author of several books,
tells of the time he "stumbled" upon his career:

> "When I was a kid, I did watch TV, but I can also remember
> a lot of time just being by myself and thinking. One
> favorite thing to do on summer days was to lie under the
> oak tree in the back yard and look up at the clouds, trying
> to see various shapes in them. It wouldn't be uncommon
> for me to spend an hour or so doing that. Another favorite
> activity was sifting through dirt pretending to look for
> gold or diamonds. I vividly remember one Saturday
> morning being outside in the chilly autumn air and feeling
> the cold, damp dirt in my hands. I was putting stones of
> different shapes in various rows, when I got an idea. I

thought, "I wonder if a person can do a job like this?" Being seven years old I had never heard of the word, geologist. When I found out there was such a thing, I couldn't believe it. I thought by thinking it first, I had somehow invented the career. Later I realized that I had luckily discovered my life's work digging in the dirt as a kid."

Parents often tell me a version of Greg's story. Perhaps it wasn't their life's path they discovered, but an important insight about themselves or a totally new understanding about the world. Free-range mental meanderings as children often influence us in important ways as adults. But even more than that, slices of daily "down time" provide wonderful opportunities to design an interior life.

Philosopher Jacob Needleman explains in his book, *Money and the Meaning of Life*, that materialism really means "we experience the external world as the strongest force in our lives... *The inner world is no longer experienced as vividly as the outer world.* The outer world begins to seem more real, more compelling, more exigent. Life in the external world begins to have more apparent *value* to the individual and the society."[2] Since an industry-generated culture with its emphasis on the material must always focus on the external in order for it to exist, it's no wonder that as a society we don't place an emphasis on the growth of an interior life. Inner qualities, like integrity, are invisible and thus can't be seen or valued as significant. Therefore, as parents we must be quite intentional in creating home and local community environments that allow our children and teens access to their inner terrain. If we want to raise children with character, it's important to remember that virtues, such as honesty, empathy, and generosity, make up the personality. They can't be imposed or taught. Rather they are birthed inside of a person when the interior life of the person reflects those qualities.

An interior life is to our minds what an enclosed porch is to our house. It's a place separate from, yet a part of the structure in which we live. It's a place to meet ourselves and have a good chat. It's a seclusion to muse and ponder. It's a timeout where we can regroup and understand ourselves better. We enter when we wish and leave when it's time. Hopefully, it's a room of light; a place where we achieve clarity and purpose.

While the first essential need of bonding with parents is the child's entry into healthy relationships, the second of the Vital Five is a necessary foundation for a healthy self-identity. Dr. Leo Buscaglia, noted author on love's power, once wrote, "Love and self are one, and the discovery of either is the realization of both."[3] Having an inner life means we can notice our own uniqueness and find the love to appreciate ourselves more fully, leading to a greater capacity to love and appreciate others. Additionally, an inner life keeps us true to who we are, enabling for self-correction when we make a mistake and pointing us in another direction to start anew. There are other gifts of an inner life and in this chapter we will explore a few. We will consider important questions as well: How does an inner life relate to a healthy self-identity? And how can we help our children design a life inside themselves in a culture that counts on them to be out of touch with their inner selves?

From Self-Recognition to Self-Regulation

Infants looking in a mirror usually see another baby, but they don't know who it is that they are seeing. Experiments have been done with young children to determine when they come to recognize themselves. Dr. C. K. Synder explains one reoccurring observation: "If one smears a small dot of red rouge on the nose of a very young child and puts a mirror in front of that child, different reactions can be expected depending on the child's age. For children under one, no special attention will be paid to the nose as seen in the mirror. Children at least one year old, however, will consistently touch their noses in the mirror and, as such, are demonstrating self-recognition skills."[4] And thus begins the journey toward self-understanding. After the baby notices his or her physical self, the path is cleared to begin the longer process of forming and knowing the inner self. Three important milestones, however, must take place in order for this to happen.

First, the young child must learn a language, or put another way, a symbolic thinking process. To express thinking so others will understand requires some form of agreed-upon communication such as a language like English or Spanish or sign language or Braille. Any form of language is actually a form of thinking using symbols. The word chair is not the actual thing. Likewise, a hand sign or a raised dotted configuration for the word "love" is not the experience itself. All languages are made up of symbols that stand for something else. The young brain starts figuring this out through daily experiences with parents. For instance, at ten months old most babies will feel some distress when Mom leaves on an errand. The child may cry or make a fuss, but can be easily distracted. Then, as many baby-sitters find out the hard way, mentioning the word, "Mommy" might easily trigger the child to look for Mommy or expect Mommy to suddenly appear. Why? At ten months, most babies have not yet separated the word, Mommy, from the actual person herself. In a few months, the child's brain matures enough to notice that Mommy is also called Helen by friends and Mrs. Smith by the UPS deliveryman. Hum. . .is this still the same Mommy? The child has every physical evidence to believe that it is, so what's going on? When Daddy calls Mommy, "Honey," and the child is also called "Honey" by both Mommy and Daddy, she has further sorting to do. And on it goes, as the words themselves then become the means for naming, not only the people around the child, but for identifying the child herself and all her personal experiences as well.

The use of language is the second important step on the journey to an inner life. Once the human brain makes this distinction between object and referent for the object, it never looks back. Rather, it moves forward to more refined uses of symbols to convey meaning. Babies go from crying to express needs, to toddlers and preschoolers who may kick to express anger, to older children who hopefully start to use words in place of anti-social behaviors. As the child starts using language in multiple contexts, she can begin to have access to her inner world. Psychologist Mihaly Csikszentmihalyi points out, "When a person has learned a symbolic system well enough to use it, she has established a portable, self-contained world within the mind."[5] Without a vocabulary, the child is constrained, not only in the outer world, but in the inner one, as well. The more words a child has, the greater the number of concepts the child's mind can hold.

Using many words with others means the child becomes able to conduct a rich inner dialogue, as well. When we adults talk to ourselves, we may think we are "losing it." But it's very human to use inner dialogue to organize our thoughts or run through in our mind a complicated issue. And sometimes verbalizing inner speech brings insight. As you read these words, tune into your inner talk. Chances are you are thinking about something else even as you think about what you are reading. It may be a past or future event. You may be relating what you are reading to a personal experience. If you are dealing with a negative emotional episode such as an argument with a spouse or a teen who has slammed a door in your face, it's almost inevitable that your mind will replay the uncomfortable emotional experience and it will be hard to concentrate.

Mature minds operate on a variety of levels. We usually have more than one track playing at any given time. We can think about what we will make for an evening dinner while listening intently to a morning lecture on personality styles. An efficient mind will know how to pay attention to what's happening in the present and not let disruptive thoughts interfere. Extraneous ideas pass through our minds like cars on a distant freeway. We hear them, but don't focus on them. If an idea has some connection to the present moment, we get a hold of it and examine it, much like a police officer pulling over a driver for questioning. In listening to that morning lecture, we will let the thought of, "Yes, I think I'll pick up shrimp for dinner tonight," walk right on by. Another thought, "Oh, what the lecturer just said makes sense. Now I know why I never liked administrative tasks—they don't fit my personality style," will take hold because it connects with the present moment. A well-tuned brain, then, acknowledges mind chatter while figuring out which thoughts are for or against us in any given situation. This is part of the brains' acquiring selective attention, a critical step for learning since it enables us to determine what's most important to pay attention to. A child without selective attention pays as much attention to another child leaving the classroom as he does the science exam in front of him. He hasn't learned to tune out minor disruptions in order to stay focused on the task at hand. In order to do that he has to have a highly sophisticated skill known as "metacognition" or thinking about one's own thinking. Meta, from the Greek word, means above. Metacognition literally means above thinking.

Metacognition is the third prerequisite to developing an inner life: a person has to be able to tune into the thoughts inside his or her head to decide if those thoughts are relevant or not. When youngsters are in play activities that require them to "talk to themselves," they are actively learning this skill. Without metacognition, it's as if a person were sitting in his enclosed porch without even knowing he was there.

One mother recently told me that school was so much of a pressure to her second-grade daughter that she had to let her come home and watch cartoons to decompress. I pointed out that a child who learns to decompress in such a way is more apt to become depressed, exhibiting lethargy instead of renewed energy. Sitting in front of a television doesn't allow for exploration of inner realms, nor does it give a child opportunities for self-discovery. Nor does it allow for kids to verbalize their thoughts, unless someone is with them asking questions. Simple activities like coloring, stretching and dancing, doing an art project, or helping with a household chore, would be better alternatives for "decompression" because they invite children to connect with their own minds in ways passive television watching can't. While actively engaging in an activity, you may hear your child talking aloud, whispering ideas, stating a plan, or blurting out a creative a-ha! By verbalizing their inner speech, youngsters organize their thinking in important ways. They are also affirming to themselves that they can think.

One learns to be inside self by being inside self. There are no other ways to do this. No short-cuts. As children develop more sophisticated language skills and amass daily activities that require them to talk within themselves, they learn how to regulate their own behaviors. When having difficulty doing a math problem, for instance, a child can say to him or herself, "OK, what do I need to figure out here? Where did I make my error? What will help me to better understand?" Instead of getting agitated, children will think through a mental challenge and persevere on their own. Rather than whining for help and feeling incapable, they will connect to mental abilities and experience the feelings of success of coming up with their own solutions. Without access to the inner world through inner speech, there is no way children can learn self-awareness, self-calming skills, or experience themselves as successful learners.

With maturity, the locus of control should move from the external stimulus to the internal choice. When this happens, the ability to postpone gratification and the ability to act more out of volition, rather than react out of emotional turmoil, emerge. When internal control is present, rationality co-exists with deeply felt emotions. Choice, more than emotional reaction, determines action. Without time to be inside self and craft an interior life, though, children can't self-regulate. They act out their strong feelings more often because they have no calming inside voice to help them out. Many "disobedient" or "defiant" children are children who have not yet acquired an interior life. They need to rely on others to control them, since they can't do it in their own heads.

Nurturing An Interior Life Leads to a Positive Self-Image

Healthy emotional development depends upon how much we like ourselves. How can children come to like who they are, if they don't spend time inside getting to know themselves? Consider the following two children, both nine years old.

> Melissa has spent three to four hours a day watching television since she was two years old. She now has a TV in her bedroom and often falls asleep with it on. Melissa dislikes school work because she can't get quick answers. She has a hard time sitting still and has started acting out in class. Melissa's teacher is concerned that she won't be well prepared for fourth grade. Her parents are thinking about getting her tested because of language delays, inappropriate classroom behaviors, and poor academic performance.

> Beth has watched one hour a day or less of television since she was three years old. Her bedroom is TV-free with lots of books. She likes to draw and has her own sketch pad. She will often sit and draw for an hour or so after school. She usually has some sort of project going. Currently she is helping her mom make a quilt for her grandmother. Beth is not an A student, but she works

hard and can sit and do her homework without need of too much help from her parents. Her teacher is pleased with Beth's efforts and her classroom behavior.

Who is growing up with a positive self-image, Melissa or Beth? Because Beth has more opportunities for self-discovery, she also has the advantage of being more in charge of herself. She is participating more fully in life than Melissa is because life is easier for her than it is for Melissa. Since Melissa's environment doesn't make it easy for her to "go inside," difficulties are compounding. As she gets tested at school and labeled as "learning deficit," her sense of self will likely further diminish. With more adults controlling her behaviors and identifying her as a "problem," how can Melissa acquire a positive self-image?

Building self-awareness and self-understanding can be strengthened at any age. While ideally the child would be on the road to a positive self-image before the age of eight, there is plenty parents can do in later childhood and during the teen years if it looks like a negative self-concept is taking hold. The key is for parents to understand the critical importance of providing opportunities. Discovering and building an interior life opens up whole new ways of being in the world and brings important insights for interacting healthily with others. We can invite children to focus on their inner selves through three basic skills that start with the letter "I," necessary for crafting a positive self-image, the "You" in each of us. I have seen minor miracles occur when parents emphasized these skills consistently:

- Introspection
- Inspiration
- Intrinsic Motivation

Introspection

When our child exclaims, "I'm bored!" often that reflects more a state of his or her self-image than actual boredom. The child isn't seeing him or herself as capable of coming up with interesting ideas. When my sons would say to me, "I'm bored," I was tempted to tell them, "A child who is bored likely will become a boring adult." But I didn't. Instead, like most mothers I would give them my fabulous ideas: How about writing that thank-you card to Grandma? What about a board game? Well, it looks like it's time to go outside." And they, of course, would reject my hopeful considerations with upturned eyes and petulant mouths. One day, when they were around seven and nine I found myself getting more irritated as they countered all my suggestions. It finally dawned on me that as I was giving them ideas of things to do, I was denying their ability to figure out their boredom in their own way. So, I said to them, "I want you to sit on that couch over there and stay bored. Yes, that's right. Just sit there. When you are done being bored, you can get up." They looked at me like I was nuts and then looked at each other as they had no alternative but to do as I said. They knew in my voice that I was fed up.

After awhile of sitting and "just thinking" they did figure something out and had fun playing an imaginative game they made up. Without this opportunity to think things through in self-reflection, I doubt if they would have come up with the game. Artists call this inside space "the fertile void," where nothing is happening, but everything is possible. Visiting it means an incubation opportunity—a vital time for the seed of a new idea to sprout. Without such introspection time, humans cripple creative expression. By going within and "just thinking," children also build resiliency skills for tackling life's demands. Sorting and sifting through inner ideas and feelings builds self-knowledge, too. Introspection is the way children can get acquainted with their interior lives. To do it optimally, though, they need "stimulus shelters."[6]

Keeping our homes quiet havens for self-reflection is a mighty challenge in our noisy, harried culture. But it's such a critical function for today's family. Important research in environmental psychology shows that too much stimulation has serious side-effects. The more overly-stimulated children get, the more likely they will have trouble sitting still to wander their mental landscape. Actually initiating time to be inside of self can seem a huge obstacle for a lot of kids. Why? Too much stimulation takes away the capacity for introspection. One fascinating study even showed that when kids have to repeatedly tune out noise in order to concentrate, they may also lose other abilities as well. Children living over a noisy highway screened out audio cues required to discriminate sounds critical for them to learn how to read. Another study showed that kids in classrooms on a noisy street had lower reading scores than kids in quieter classrooms.[7] Music or TV also drain energy and focus away from intended purposes. A study measured the effect of music and television on sixth grade and college students' reading performance on a standardized reading test. It was interesting that most people thought that the music was the most difficult to have on while reading and that the television being on had not bothered their performance too much. However, the results were just the opposite. In fact, the reading performance of the sixth graders was two grade levels lower with the music on and four years lower with the TV on. The college students performed one and a half grades worse with the music on and two years worse with the TV on. The author of this study concluded, "Apparently, although we are able as humans to do some things well at the same time, we are not able to effectively read and either listen to something or watch something at the same time. Students should not study with radio or the television on if they wish to do their best work."[8]

Time in front of televisions or video games doesn't count as introspection time, either. They are too stimulating to low brain sensibilities. With bright colored images, often fast-paced flashes, they actually distract the child from having his or her own thoughts. Some teens can manage to travel their inner paths while listening to music, but often they are immersed in the lyrics and not discovering their own inner voices. Working on a computer can be a wonderful thinking adventure. But too much time with computers also distracts kids from their inner selves. A therapist friend of mine laments the effect of overuse of computers in childhood. She has a ten year-old client with carpal tunnel syndrome because he spends about five hours a day on the computer, almost every minute he is not in school or sleeping. She explains, "What is so sad is that this boy has no emotional affect at all. There's no joy or curiosity in his eyes. He is withdrawn and socially inept. All he wants is to be on the computer. He eats dinner alone in front of the computer and will only do his homework if promised more computer time."

It would be important to know what this boy is actually doing on the computer. Is he composing poetry or writing an interesting research paper? If he were in these creative endeavors, he would be drawing upon his interior life and feeding it as well. Chances are, like too many children today, he spends computer time in easy games or surfing the Internet. It's difficult for humans to become addicted to using mental functions or creating something new. Rather, we form addictions to activities that don't require us to bring much of ourselves to the activity. The very nature of an addiction is that the person is unconscious of the detrimental effects of his or her pursuits. Not being fully present in the activity, the activity controls the person, rather than vice versa. Entering the worlds created by software developers, computer programmers, or video game designers means that kids don't have to give much of themselves to the process in which they engage. It's all been done for them. They can play the game well, unaware of their inner selves. Writing in *Party of One*, Anneli Rufus points out, "Computer and video games are most often played alone…solo protagonists playing these games dispatch villains, solve problems, and blow things to bits. But the player hardly needs to think, only to click. Hours go by in a kind of daze. The child has not created a unique character, story, or situation…Playing this way he is cut off even from himself."[9] When children are given opportunities to be able to be "inside themselves" without need of any external stimulation, they come to value their own thinking processes and capabilities in important ways. Too much time with externalized images on screens prevent children and teens from knowing themselves. And, they can't value what they don't know.

Rufus' book is subtitled *The Loner's Manifesto*. She makes an important distinction between a true loner who values self and others, and a person who sees him or herself as an outcast and then sets himself apart from others. Children, who by their nature are shy or introverted, may be true loners. But they may get pushed into participating. Parents can panic that the child may be a budding sociopath if he or she would rather be alone. Rufus writes, "You would think parents would be pleased with a child capable of entertaining him or herself. Think of the advantages. Such a child learns to be resourceful, independent, learns to concentrate...Solo pastimes hone creativity. Reading. Writing. Crafts. Acting out dramas in which the lone player must devise the plot, portray every character, come up with costumes and a denouement. You would think parents would appreciate this. You'd think they'd be grateful. But they're not. Parents today are too well-versed in tales of friendless children who grow into murderers...the bully or the sad-sack outcast is not the same as the child who chooses to play solo games. The first two have a problem. The loner has no friends or few friends not because of failure or bad behavior but because he chooses so carefully. Loners can play well with others, the right others..."[10] Healthy introspection shouldn't be confused with anti-social withdrawal.

Simple Ways Parents Can Encourage Introspection

Children no longer live in a nineteenth century *Secret Garden* world where they amble through nature in walled-off comfort. Therefore, we have to figure out how to provide opportunities for introspection within an extremely distracting culture. Like any skill, introspection can be learned when practiced. Here are ways that work:

- *Take a day on the weekend for a family inventory.* Are there changes that can be made such as a rule to limit blaring music after a certain hour? Find out what works for family members to spend quiet time "inside their heads." Discuss how you can help each other gain time and space for introspection by being more aware of each others' needs.

- *Provide a special place for "quiet thinking."* It may be an overstuffed chair in the living room or a kitchen nook. Maybe you will create one with a few pillows in a corner of the rec room. Wherever it is, when a child (or parent) is there, it means, "Please do not talk to me. I am taking a mental journey away from it all. Be back soon."

- *Keep the TV off when no one is watching it.* This isn't healthy "background noise." Rather it contributes to children's perceptual chaos. Kids won't go inside easily with the TV replacing the focus of attention.

- *Invite "think-links."* These are times to link with one's own thinking. As a classroom teacher, I used to have my students put their heads down on their desks and "just think about" a question I asked for five minutes before raising their hands. When helping your child with homework, you can do the same. When frustration mounts and answers don't come readily have your son or daughter close eyes and do a "think-link." With your child calmed down, ask one question that might get your child headed in the right direction. Give him at least five minutes to think about the question. Don't talk about anything at this time. After the thinking time is up, discuss any insights or ideas your child has come up with. Observe how he or she links to own thinking given a time-out to do so.

- *Ask the question, "What are you saying to yourself about_____?"* This is a handy question to ask when reading aloud to children or when they are reading to you. For teens, it's an excellent question when they are in a dilemma, not sure which choice to make. It opens up self-knowledge and an opportunity for us as parents to peek into how their minds are operating and make course corrections as needed.

- *State the sentence, "I see you need to think about that a bit."* When our children want us to make a quick decision for them, this is an excellent opportunity to give them a chance to reflect upon what they're asking. Similar things we could say are: "Why don't you reflect on what you just said for the rest of the day, and then let's talk about it tonight?" Or "I like the way you are taking time to think this through."

Inspiration

While introspection helps kids value themselves, inspiration enables kids to value their capacity to come up with ideas. When was the last time you felt inspired? Think back upon a time when you encountered illumination. Whether you were struck with just the right way to fix a leaky gutter, or captured the exact colors on a canvas, chances are these moments also connected you to a positive sense of self. A can-do attitude springs forth and we feel good about what we can accomplish.

What's inspiring out there for our kids in the industry-generated culture? When we look around we see superficiality, nihilistic attitudes, messages that shout we are terminally deprived, a quasi-human if we don't measure up to an arbitrary industry-generated standard. Rather than seeing this as the ultimate lie, a lot of kids absorb these messages as gospel truth—not a way to induce inspiration by any means. In a commodified culture such as ours, it seems we parents need a lot of inspiration to figure out how to help our kids experience inspiration!

Perhaps the best way is the simplest. When our kids go with an idea or produce something, we can help them get acquainted with the impetus behind their creations. When a young child runs to us and says, "Look Mommy, see what I did," we can pick up his drawing and say, "That's beautiful. I can see that you were inspired." When our ninth grader works hard to score a goal for her team, afterwards we can comment, "That was some inspiring play out there." When our high school senior has to write his college application essay and is in a panic because he can't think of anything, we can reassure with, "Just take some time, inspiration will come, it always does. You know that. Be patient and trust it." When we identify inspiring moments for our kids and affirm their ability to be inspired they will have faith that it will show up when needed. And it will.

Intrinsic Motivation

Inspiration will naturally lead to children and teens capable of motivating themselves. This may seem like a surprising statement given the tremendous amount of resources that go into prodding kids to function in our schools. It's as if we have lost all trust in their commitment to learn and we have taken up "the burden" for them. Joy in discovery, satisfaction in accomplishment, and enthusiasm in creativity are sadly missing from too many children's experiences—either at school or at home. For these qualities to be present in learning experiences, humans must be motivated from the inside out. Yes, external rewards play a part in determining our choices. Few people will work forty hours a week without a paycheck. But most want those forty hours to be meaningful to them in some way. Unless we are also intrinsically motivated, our activities are void of meaning and purpose.

Jon was a fourteen year-old boy who couldn't be inspired easily. His parents came to me very disheartened as they had "tried everything," but Jon was still failing school. More than that, Jon was failing himself. He hadn't read a book since third grade. He came home from school and played video games for three hours and he refused to do any schoolwork. His parents were at their wits' end with Jon's resistance. The more they pushed, the more he refused to do anything. He was smart and creative, but read at a fifth grade level. He had no special needs; no learning disabilities. What Jon lacked was will.

Tutoring Jon proved challenging because any work I gave him to do, he didn't do it. I enlisted the support of his parents and we kept video games to three hours on weekends. Jon had to read for an hour when he came home from school, then aloud another hour to his parents after he did his homework. He had some serious catching up to do. For awhile, I was able to motivate Jon by talking with him about his many talents. I asked him what he liked to do and he said, "Write scripts." So he wrote a script on a subject of his choice. But learning to read more complex material like social studies texts proved arduous and Jon wasn't up to the task. Every week he would tell me that "he couldn't do it," when asked about the assignments I had given him. Intellectually, of course, he could. But he didn't know that about himself. How could I get him to believe in himself again?

Baby steps of tapping into what Jon was willing to do proved key. Together we discovered that he enjoyed taking care of his dog, so he read books on dog care and eventually the history of dogs and how they influence human behavior. That led him to some research on dogs and eventually cats. Over a six month period Jon started to engage in his other readings and in the assignments I gave him. A spark was lit. One afternoon session, Jon casually looked at me and asked, "What courses would I need to take in high school to become a veterinarian?" My jaw didn't drop to the floor because I was smiling instead. Jon had connected to a purpose inside of himself. He thought he might be interested in becoming a veterinarian. All of a sudden, the schoolwork didn't look so bad. He was able to deal with its difficulty because, inspired by a vision of what could be, he became intrinsically motivated to see if he could make it happen.

Inner motivation emerges out of various interactions that keep the child or teen focused on his or her strong core inside. In compiling the research, I have identified five components of intrinsic motivation—capacity, choice, challenge, control, and creativity. Each is determined by an internal quality.

The capacity for being motivated internally is determined by a person's *self-image.* Children who grow up liking themselves within a loving, supportive home environment are more apt to use an inner guidance system for figuring out what interests them. They rely less on what others think and more on what they themselves want. Their desires spring forth from felt needs or urges and they can't be easily tempted with bribes. Strong within themselves, people with a healthy self-image don't need to earn "a reward" to feel good. Rather they derive feelings of pleasure and satisfaction from doing something they want, something that, for them, has significance. Before Jon could make any progress, for instance, we had to work with him on changing his self-image so that he could develop the needed capacity to be intrinsically motivated by something.

Choosing intrinsic motivation seems to be evident in a person's level of *self-awareness*. Children who learn their unique likes and dislikes have more choices for what inspires them. When they come to value their individuality, they can decide for or against doing something based on what will truly be interesting to them. Offering children and teens a wide variety of experiences helps them get in touch with what they can be successful doing. These activities will naturally be motivating to them. The more Jon came to know himself, the more he selected books that interested him, leading him to deeper insights about what was important to him.

The degree of challenge people will deal with when intrinsically motivated is seen in their level of *self-determination*. Will a child choose an easy, known puzzle or go for the new one, slightly more difficult? With strong determination, a child can choose the harder activity because he knows he will persist with it. Working through a difficulty, while a challenge, doesn't become a frustrating, impossible task. The more a child or teen will embrace a challenge, the more likely intrinsic motivation for learning something new will be strengthened. Once Jon amazed himself by reading books of greater complexity, he became more determined to keep challenging himself and more willing to try new challenges.

People will control their intrinsically motivated experiences to the degree that those experiences are *self-directed*. When we do something just for the sake of doing it, we are in charge of the experience. We don't want anyone else to control it. In his now classic book, *Punished by Rewards*, Alfie Kohn explains it this way: "...imagine that you have given your next-door neighbor a ride downtown, or some help moving a piece of furniture, and that he then offers you five dollars for your trouble. If you feel insulted by the gesture, consider why this should be, what the payment implies."[11] Kohn goes on to discuss the power differential between the giver of the reward and the receiver of the reward. By being offered a reward for doing something that we really want to do, we can feel controlled. "...rewarding someone emphasizes the rewarder's position of greater power."[12] It's so important to let our kids engage in an experience that they self-direct for no other reason than to have the experience. In a sense a reward cheapens the experience for them. Children build competence and autonomy when they self-direct their behaviors.[13] With external controls or rewards, they can't learn to trust their inner voices or be comfortable with their choices. Jon had to find his own way out of his lack of motivation. When I and his parents set firm boundaries, but also allowed Jon to direct some of his learning experiences, it paved the way for Jon to be more in control of his own learning.

Creating from a sense of internal drive is determined by a person's level of *self-actualization*. In other words, people who spend much of their time coming up with new ideas or creating new ways of doing things are said to be "self-actualizing," a word coined by psychologist Abraham Maslow. Self-actualizing people know they can rely on themselves to come up with the answers they will need. Children and teens in touch with their interior lives will celebrate their creativity and naturally seek out new learning experiences for ever growing self-actualization. Jon entered high school with a creative purpose, feeling that he could accomplish his own self-chosen goal.

Components of Intrinsic Motivation

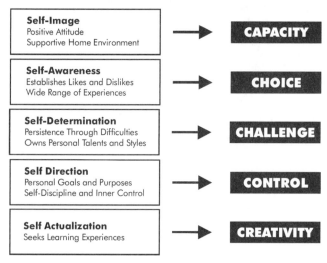

Self-Image Positive Attitude Supportive Home Environment	**CAPACITY**
Self-Awareness Establishes Likes and Dislikes Wide Range of Experiences	**CHOICE**
Self-Determination Persistence Through Difficulties Owns Personal Talents and Styles	**CHALLENGE**
Self Direction Personal Goals and Purposes Self-Discipline and Inner Control	**CONTROL**
Self Actualization Seeks Learning Experiences	**CREATIVITY**

An Inner Life Helps a Child Feel Included

One of the paradoxes of humans is that the more confident they are in themselves and not in need of people, the more people seek them out and the more they are included within the group. Also, a person with a healthy self-image is inclusive and can reach out to others, even becoming effective group leaders. These by-products of spending time inside oneself are not often recognized. In our society, we place a great value on socializing our youngsters, arranging "play dates," making sure children know how to get along with their peers. As our kids get older, they usually are involved in after school activities that expand their choice of friends beyond the classroom. This is all fine and certainly necessary, to a point. But children who do not develop an interior life will be less capable of successfully relating to their peers.

It's brutal out there for many kids. Meanness has always been around and there have always been bullies, drumming up trouble. But the frequency and the increasing brutality that is occurring today is unprecedented. Bullying occurs on school playgrounds every seven minutes and once every twenty-five minutes in class.[14] Taunting, teasing, and spreading rumors on-line is a new form of "cyber-bullying." One in seventeen kids, ages ten to seventeen, have been threatened or harassed online and about one-third of those found the incidents "extremely distressing" according to a study by the University of New Hampshire's Crimes Against Children Research Center.[15] Debra Pepler and Wendy Craig have been studying bullying for over twenty-five years. Their extensive research has caused them to conclude "We believe that bullying, the combined use of power and aggression, is a problem throughout the lifespan. Children do not 'just grow out of it.' On the contrary, we believe that children who learn how to acquire power through aggression on the playground may transfer these lessons to sexual harassment, date violence, gang attacks, marital abuse, child abuse, and elder abuse."[16]

It's important to remember that kind acts or sharing toys don't come easily to toddlers and many young children. It doesn't mean they are on a course to becoming bullies and shouldn't be labeled as such. In a cross-cultural study in the early 1960s, Eibl-Eibesfeldt found "toddlers...hitting, kicking, biting and spitting at one another" no matter what culture studied. It was unlikely the children learned these behaviors from parents or from television. Most of the parents worked hard to teach and model socially acceptable behaviors. In many of the countries television was not yet available, so the youngsters were not imitating screen violence. This research led some theorists to conclude that "the behavioral circuitry of sadism seems a curse genetically prestamped into us."[19] For parents of young children this translates into not forcing friendships. By allowing the young child to learn how to play by him or herself, the child's brain develops a few more cognitive circuits that will assist in curbing acting out when with other children. It also means that when toddlers are with other children, any violent behaviors are re-directed into intense physical activities like jumping on big pillows. Also, spending more time on mother's lap or on dad's shoulders and experiencing the limbic resonance I discussed in Chapter Three can really assist toddlers' in controlling aggressiveness or impulsivity. When youngsters become mobile and heavier, many parents don't hold them as often as they did when infants. If your toddler is "out of control" try more closeness and shared experiences. Try teaching your toddler how to play by him or herself. These could really help to spur a toddler's self-understanding and better prepare the youngster for time with friends.

Designing an interior life can re-direct a potential bully and empower a potential victim. As children of all ages get in touch with themselves, they also tap their personal power. They have less need to prove themselves to others because they have internal proof that they are capable beings. Nurturing an inner self opens children and teens to their potential to include themselves with others. Since they can't separate from themselves, they bring to socialization a "built-in" inclusion mentality. They sense they already belong to the world because their sense of self is growing appropriately.

Parents can make the interrelatedness between developing an inner life and being included with friends more conscious to kids. Here are some example statements you could say to your child:

With Younger Children

- Time alone right now can help you learn what you like best. Then you can share that with _____ when she comes over to play.
- I like the way you are learning to play by yourself. That helps you learn to play better with others.
- When you play quietly by yourself, you are getting ready to play well with your friends.
- When you sit and think you can come up with ideas to play nicely with your friends.

With Older Children and Teens

- When you think inside yourself, you discover who you are. This will make you a better friend.
- Think about how you want to invite your friends to the party, then let's talk about it.
- You participate in groups very well, did you know that? Why don't you ponder your many talents for interacting with a group? I can name several talents you have. I'll share them with you after you had time to come up with some yourself.
- The more you know yourself, the more you can offer in friendship to others, so the time in self-reflection is well-spent.

The Other Word that Begins with the Letter "I"

There is another important component of designing an interior life. In fact, it's so important we will be spending Chapter Five examining it—image making, the third essential human need.

Your Inner Life Can Fuel Your Parenting

The greatest parental challenge from my own experience and from what most parents tell me is finding time for ourselves. This can mean time to unwind after work, or with our spouses having a quiet dinner together, with friends to chat and catch up, or time for a quick shower or a luxurious, long bath. Moments like these are sometimes hard to come by—but so essential for providing the stamina one needs for the demands of parenting. And really a necessity in order to draw from our parenting well.

Why not make a commitment to yourself right now as you finish this chapter to give yourself the gifts of Introspection, Inspiration, and Intrinsic Motivation each day? Here's how it could work:

1. Intentionally commit to these three skills of an inner life by printing the words on a 3X5 card. Keep the card where you will see it regularly.

2. As you go about your day, ask yourself three questions. Print these questions on the back of the card:
   Can I find five minutes (or more) to be inside myself and just think? (Introspection)
   Can I connect inside to any inspiring ideas that bring positive, hopeful feelings? (Inspiration)
   Can I find something I am motivated to do out of sheer joy? (Intrinsic Motivation)

3. If you can find time for Introspection, Inspiration, and Intrinsic Motivation, great! If not all three, maybe one today and one or two tomorrow? No push. No rush. Just take a step each day to feed your inner life, knowing quite sure it will fuel your parenting.

When we help our children develop their interior lives, there's an added bonus for us because as they grow they will be more apt to be responsible for themselves. That means less direction from us, ultimately. Having self-determined children means we will have more time and energy to devote to ourselves and to our parenting. Our children don't drain our energy when they have an interior life. So many parents I meet are over-working to "get their kids" to do something whether it's homework or housework. Or they are overburdened by "getting their kids not to do something," whether it's bullying on the playground or bugging their sibling. Let's face it. Trying to help a person who is not intrinsically motivated is like pushing a rock up hill. But helping a person who is intrinsically motivated is like guiding the direction of a rock as it meanders down a hill. There's a lot less energy involved. As we nurture the growth of our children's interiority, we have more time and energy to value our own. As our awareness of our own interior life grows, we can share insights gained with our children and celebrate together the benefits of an inner life. Building on the limbic resonance of a shared, emotional life, we find tapping into our parent well a natural, nurturing process— for us and our children.

To Cultivate Your Inner Life

Each of us has to find that rhythm throughout the day that enables us to have some time inside ourselves and enough time to do all that we have to do. Use the statements here (from parents I have worked with) as ways to assess what might work best for you to cultivate your inner life.

- I must have a few minutes in the morning before the kids get up to be with myself. I nurse that first cup of coffee very slowly.

- Before bedtime, I really appreciate having a half-hour all to myself to read and unwind after my daughter is in bed.

- I find that I have my best visits with myself on my walks or while working out at the gym.

- There are times when I just have to put the "Do not disturb sign" on my door and let my husband handle things for awhile.

- It's really important for me to have regular time just meandering the neighborhood shops and wonderful little galleries.

- I find that occasionally I will go to the library without the kids. I sit there for a time, read a magazine or the newspaper and then pick up some books to bring home to them.

- I have a friend I call and she comes over and spends time with the kids. I can take off on errands, get a latte, and stare into space for fifteen minutes, blessedly alone.

5
The Third Essential Need: Image Making

It is the capacity for organizing information into larger and complex images which is the chief glory of our species.

Kenneth E. Boulding[1]

The gray skies and chilly afternoon drizzle were a stark contrast to the light and warmth of the cozy classroom where forty teachers had gathered with me to discuss "Teaching in a Media Age." This particular workshop was memorable not only because of the wonderful people I met, but because I heard the following story from a second grade teacher:

> "I started reading aloud to the class after lunch on the first day of school, like I always do. All of the children were in rapt attention, with the exception of one little boy. I walked over to him and asked, 'What's the matter? Are you OK?' He was fidgeting and seemed agitated. He looked at me blankly and whispered anxiously, 'What am I supposed to do?' I replied, 'Well, I'd like you to listen to the story.' He seemed confused. So I continued, 'We are

quiet now and enjoying the story I'm reading.' He still didn't understand. We talked back and forth for awhile until I got an inkling of what was going on for this child. I finally asked, 'Tommy, don't you see pictures in your head when I'm reading aloud?' He shook his head, 'No, should I?'"

This was the first time I heard of such a response from a child, but since then I've heard it from other teachers around the country. Not being able to make up "pictures in your head" while listening to a story seems foreign to most of us. But the capacity to make up inner images from spoken words must be practiced in order to be developed. Are children in a media age growing up without using much of their image making capacities? The number of industry-generated images literally staggers the imagination. Watching a two-hour video brings in over 2,000 images—all created by someone else. Millions of children absorb countless television images daily. The visual image appears on roadside billboards, town bulletin boards, and magazines. Even school textbooks are becoming more image-focused with less print and more brightly-colored graphics. It's estimated that a U. S. child will be exposed to at least 1,000 visual images throughout an average day.

With so many external pictures available, where does that leave our image making capacities as humans? In an industry-generated culture that relies heavily on visual images to convey its repetitive messages, many children and teens can lose sight of their own image making capabilities. Without an understanding of themselves as image makers, kids can also lose sight of their ability to generate their own messages. Then they can get confused into thinking that the external industry-generated visual messages are their own. How do we help our kids value and understand the importance of their image making capacities when the industry-generated culture promotes the opposite? As a society we are not close to understanding the power of images. Like goldfish oblivious to their water environment, many parents today don't see our current visual environment and what it's doing to their kids' behaviors and choices. Dismissing the obvious, they look to mechanistic solutions like drugs to deal with children's attention deficit, depression, or hyperactivity. Parents can't be blamed for not understanding how nurturing image making capacities in their children could help these conditions. The information necessary for different, more human parental decisions is just not "out there."

In this chapter we will address these issues and provide practical tools that will enhance your child's brain functioning by nurturing image-making capabilities. We will look at what images are, what they do, and how children learn to make them. And we will explore ways to support this third essential need for our children's optimal development, as well as for our own parental well-being.

What are Images?
What Do They Do?
How Do Children Learn to Make Them?

We usually think of a visual representation when we hear the word "image," but images inside the human brain are more than that. Internationally recognized neuroscientist Antonio Damasio defines an image as a "mental pattern." It seems that the human brain excels at putting together patterns that form all sorts of images. Explains Damasio, "The word image does not refer to 'visual' image alone…The word also refers to sound images such as those caused by music or wind and to the…images that Einstein used in his mental problem solving…Images in all modalities 'depict' processes…of all kinds, concrete as well as abstract." In other words, Damasio adds, "Thought is an acceptable word to denote…a flow of images."[2]

In his seminal book *Evolution's End*, Joseph Chilton Pearce agrees with Damasio's definition. He writes: "images are a primary part of thought. We think through imagery. Even congenitally blind people think in images. Congenitally blind teenagers were…found to have more accurate internal imaging than seeing teenagers, as well as a more creative and constructive imagination."[3] How is that possible? It has to do with the ability of the brain to "bypass the eye" to form mental patterns.[4] Through touch, taste, smell and hearing, images can be formed and the imagination spurred. Understanding exactly how the brain produces non-visual "images" is probably best left up to brain researchers. As parents, what's important for us to focus on is the enormous role image making plays in optimal brain functioning.

Since image making involves many parts of the brain, it's paramount to all of our thinking processes. Images weave a tapestry of thought and feeling that enable us to integrate knowledge with experiences. Our mental images also provide an impetus to action. They influence both behaviors and decisions. Images do a lot. Without them we are less capable and less creative. Einstein once said, "Imagination is more important than knowledge." He knew what he was talking about. The ground floor of knowledge lies in our image-making capacities.

Image making provides access to the symbolic functions of

our brain. We think in concrete terms, and we think abstractly. An image isn't something we can taste or hold. It's an abstraction. People with high degrees of image making abilities such as poets, mathematicians, and musicians are also people who are comfortable with abstract thought. Studies reveal that when faced with extreme physical deprivation these types of people were able to discover new pathways out of their situations better than unimaginative people.[5] In his book *Flow*, Mihaly Csikszentmihalyi describes how an imagination helps unlock problem solving. "Whenever the outside world offers no mercy," he writes, "an internal symbolic system can become a salvation. Anyone in possession of portable rules for the mind has a great advantage."[6] We only have to think of people who have survived extreme weather conditions or escaped a tyrant by their wits to see how inexorably linked image making is to our capacity to think and solve problems innovatively. But we don't have to be under severe survival conditions to benefit from our image making abilities. The on-going gifts of imaginative thought can turn everyday events into extraordinary experiences because we can think our way through daily challenges.

Image making orchestrates thinking processes while allowing us an entry into "possibility thinking." The more we are capable of accessing our image making abilities, the more fully alive we can be. Children and teens, in touch with their image-making abilities, are much more likely to be successful in school and to be better able to successfully navigate the industry-generated culture. They will enjoy visual entertainment, for example, without being manipulated by it. The beautiful images in a movie such as *Finding Nemo* for young children, or a movie such as *The Lord of the Rings* trilogy for teens, can inspire and provoke positive self-expression when kids leave the multi-plexes. When children of all ages understand that the set-designer, the camera people, and the art director played roles in generating poignant external visual images, they can come to respect image making abilities, not only in filmmakers, but also in themselves. Too often, though, most kids don't think of themselves as equal to those creative people who make wonderful visual images for our enjoyment. But in terms of brain potential, our children have the same capacity as anyone else. Csikszentmihalyi makes a critical point when he writes that "people without an internalized symbolic system can all too easily become captives of the media. They are easily manipulated by demagogues, pacified by entertainers, and exploited by anyone who has something to sell."[7] With use of their own imaginations, rather than becoming captives of the media, our kids can be creators of their own positive media experiences, capable of critically analyzing any visual image they see.

But children will only be able to do this if their image making capacities are developed. The critical time for this development is in infancy and early childhood. Young humans learn to make internal images in essentially two ways: by listening to language and by practicing through play.

Image Making by Listening to Language

The boy mentioned in the story at the beginning of the chapter may not have been exposed to enough verbal language while a toddler and a preschooler. His capacity to translate what he hears into an internally constructed mental image was weak or perhaps non-existent. In a media age, this is a serious concern. Joseph Chilton Pearce points out that "television floods the infant-child brain with images at the very time his or her brain is supposed to learn to make images from within."[8] Because the ability to make images forms the basis of other thinking processes, failure to learn how to generate internal images means much more than having no imagination. Pearce has elegantly explained what is lost to children who overuse external screen images at the expense of under using their own:

> "Failing to develop imagery means...children who can't 'see' what the mathematical symbol or the semantic words mean, nor the chemical formulae, nor the concept of civilization as we know it. They can't comprehend the subtleties of our Constitution or Bill of Rights and are seriously...bored by abstractions of this sort. They can sense only what is immediately bombarding their physical system and are restless and ill-at-ease without such bombardment. Being sensory deprived they initiate stimulus through constant movement...Having no inner imaging capacity leaves most of the brain unemployed, and a child who can't imagine not only can't learn but has no hope in general. He or she can't 'imagine' an inner scenario to replace the outer one, so feels victimized by the environment...unimaginative children are far more prone to violence than imaginative children, because they can't imagine an alternative when direct sensory information is threatening, insulting, unpleasant, or unrewarding. They lash out against unpleasantness in typical R-system [reptilian system] defensiveness, while the imaginative child can imagine an alternative, that is, create images...that offer a way out...imagination gives resiliency, flexibility, endurance, and the capacity to forgo immediate reward on behalf of long-term strategies."[9]

To reap all these rewards of image making, the young child must make up images internally by listening to language. In our overly-visual world, auditory input gets shortchanged. So the first thing parents must do is to make sure youngsters are hearing rich stories about the human condition more often than they are seeing industry-generated pictures. With TV, video, or computer games, a picture is linked to any language that is heard. Visual images dominate spoken words, especially with children whose own language abilities and vocabulary are not yet developed. When children listen to a story being read aloud by a parent or from an audio recording, they must listen carefully without the distraction of the visual image. This is a critical brain exercise. By taking in words and sentences that form a coherent story, the child continually makes up mental imagery. As Jeffrey Scheuer writes in his book *The Sound Bite Society*, "written narrative engages the mind in projecting its own internal images."[10] This can't happen in front of a screen machine.

In a world awash with visual information, we can't escape the fact that the human brain is essentially a symbolic brain. It makes up symbols so readily that one scholar has written that the "universality of symbol learning across a wide spectrum of circumstances indicate that the human brain has been significantly over-built for learning symbolic associations…We are not just adapted for symbol learning, but for *fail-safe symbol learning.*"[11] Symbol learning takes place when a child listens to a book being read aloud. During this process, the symbols of the language are reconstructed in the child's mind into pictures. Learning to interpret symbols is the work of the young brain. Listening to music, learning a first and second language, and being introduced to mathematical concepts such as addition and subtraction are other ways parents of young children can encourage symbol learning. Before the age of eight, children are primed for symbol learning. If you were to go away from reading this book with one idea of what would make the biggest difference in your child's life, this would be it:

Read to your child at least a half-hour every day. Make sure audio tapes and CDs of books, stories, poetry, folk tales, and myths and legends are readily available. Play word games, sing songs, rhymes, chants often. Make up dialogues for lots of puppet play. Discuss books, ideas, opinions around the dinner table every night. Tell many stories— real and made-up ones. Immerse your child in listening to language. You will not regret it. When children are read to often and have daily experiences listening to language, they do well in school, are capable of self-control and self-direction, and express their ideas and feelings coherently.

Literal Pictures	Symbolic Language
Evokes R-system emotional reactions	Can aid the brain in tempering R-system
Requires no use of imagination	Engages and employs imagination
Requires no mental effort	Requires mental effort
Can influence subconsciously	More conscious thought needed

Image Making Through Play

Pretend play is the way young children practice turning internal images into actions. By taking on different roles, for instance, they absorb various image-sets of feelings, attitudes, and actions. When children play, they enter the realm of the imaginal, the world of the artist and poet. This world is their home. Through play experiences, children plan and organize, predict and anticipate, take risks, reflect and experiment. Without these types of experiences, image making doesn't develop into a self-chosen activity.

Decades of empirical research has established the multiple benefits of children's imaginative play. Because image making forms the basis for thought and because the young brain naturally seeks symbolic experiences, play develops cognitive, emotional, and social learning. Research has found that it also "fosters an impressive array of skills that are necessary for school success including taking another's perspective, regulating one's emotions, taking turns with peers, sequencing the order of events, and recognizing one's independence from others."[12] Not surprisingly, children who engage regularly in imaginative play are more creative than their peers and often leaders in their peer group. Rather than forcing young children into an academic mold early with worksheets, structured games, and computer-based learning, parents would be wise to follow a more brain-compatible approach: Just let youngsters play.

In our industry-generated culture, however, we have to accurately describe what kind of play parents should foster. That play is called generative play.

Reproductive and Generative Images

There are two distinct forms of image making—reproductive and generative. Everyone has both capacities. For instance, we reproduce or imitate what we see other people say or do. It may be local slang expressions. A lot of us imitate our parents' ways of doing things. We may mimic a friend's speech patterns or a role-model's philosophy. Human beings are like copy machines in this way.

When we put together a recipe based on several favorites, when we write an original poem, make up a song, or figure out how to stay within a budget, however, we are using a generative imagination. Taking bits of this experience and that experience, combining past and present knowledge, making some future estimates, and adding it all together to make something new. It may be similar to someone else's, but it can't be exactly the same. Our new creation has been made possible because we went beyond mere reproduction of something we have seen or heard to employing a wide array of internal images to generate something unique, something only we could create, something relevant to our own life.

A young child taking in four to five hours a day of industry-generated images can come to rely more on a reproductive imagination than on a generative one. Preschoolers, for instance, imitate their favorite action heroes very well. They are masters at reproductive imagination, rattling off the same script as cartoon characters, performing TV-character body movements perfectly, and basically confining their play to what they have seen. They do this at the expense of practicing their generative image making abilities. Using only a reproductive imagination is extremely limiting. For healthy play that promotes healthy humans, children must bring in real-world experiences into their play scenarios. Added to what the child has seen on television, then, there might be characters the child made up from books someone has read to him, plot ideas from Grandfather's stories, and dialogue from something he overheard while at the library. Instead of merely mimicking external television, movie, or video images, now the child is using internally-generated images to create a personalized play experience.

Using various images from the real-world in their play is absolutely necessary for children to grow up emotionally healthy. The fact that many children *only* imitate what they see on TV for their pretend play is a cause for widespread alarm and significant intervention methods. By practicing reproduction of industry-generated messages day in and day out, without role-playing other experiences, the child becomes a commodified vessel. Industry-generated images and feelings saturate his self-identity. It's not surprising that the child's choices begin to align with these predominate inner pictures. It becomes easier, then, to kick and shove because the inner mental model the child holds is one of kicking and shoving. Having practiced these behaviors in play, they become second-nature as the child's emotional range is limited to an aggressive, anti-social model.

When Jerome Bruner, a well-respected cognitive psychologist, made the following statement in 1975, I doubt whether he knew he was giving parents of the 21st century a warning: "Play is the serious business of childhood…it's how a child learns society's rule systems for social restraint."[13] But this is only true if children are imitating images of people demonstrating social restraint. Back in 1975, it was just assumed that children imitate the positive adult roles around them and then make up their own play from a broad-base of experiences. Not so today. Play is still the serious business of childhood. But we have to differentiate between imitative play based solely on acting out industry-generated images and generative play based on images that are self-constructed from diverse experiences. What Bruner didn't have to consider in 1975 was that by imitating anti-social, or even deviant images, the young child can no longer be expected to absorb appropriate feeling states to learn social restraint and make healthy decisions in a social context. Rather, the child learns to push, shove, and kick. Hurting other people or dominating through force becomes an almost unconscious decision. If a child's play centers around negative images, the child's proclivities are reinforced rather than redirected. Continually imitating such behaviors, the child is trapped in an abyss of a repetitive, limited emotional repertoire. He becomes distanced from his internal image making processes. And it's a long climb out.

The industry-generated culture gives young children images of the adult world before the child has constructed an adult framework of meaning and before the child has acquired a corresponding experience base. Children do not have the capacity to adequately interpret the image-mediated information, nor can they evaluate the personal significance of the information. If youngsters don't get inappropriate images explained to them by caring adults or if they receive the wrong information about the images, they learn attitudes, behaviors, even feelings that may take a long time to repair. Early childhood professor Alice Sterling Hoing provides a compelling example:

> "'There was a guy and he raped this girl on the TV last night,' cheerfully reported Matt, four years old, to his day care teacher. She murmured, 'How terrible! That must have hurt the girl and scared her awfully.' 'Oh, no,' assured Matt, 'my sister's boyfriend was watching with us and he said that girls love rape. You just don't know about that,' the four-year-old responded in superior tones."[14]

With this kind of skewed information, how will this boy interpret to himself the concept of rape? Will his ideas about rape become part of his fantasy play?

Play, biologically and socially, didn't evolve as entertainment. Rather, play for young humans is an integral part of learning what it means to be humans. Generative play experiences based on appropriate models, therefore, enable children to try on a wide range of human behaviors. The child may pretend to be an anti-social TV character for a part of the play, but he or she also would take on some pro-social roles as well—perhaps as a grocery store clerk, a school bus driver, a gardener, or a teacher. Real-life roles like these would spur a wide-range of appropriate feeling states and help the child learn how to deal with the inappropriate feeling states learned from imitating unacceptable television models. Brain research underlines the critical importance of diverse emotional experiences for a healthy self-concept. Joseph LeDoux, Professor of Science at New York University's Center for Neural Science, puts it this way, "the broader the range of emotions that a child experiences, the broader will be the emotional range of the self that develops."[15] A play experience based on real-life people necessitates that the child will become various ordinary people in addition to action super heroes. Inventing as they go, children naturally happen upon lots of different feelings because they play different characters. This requires them to practice important decision-making skills from a variety of perspectives and a wide range of feeling states.

Another important factor is the development of the ability to initiate actions through fantasy play. This is a critical stage of youngsters' development outlined in Erik Erickson's stage theory. Erickson demonstrated that between the ages of three and five, children use fantasy play to learn how to engage their world.[16] But by play acting the latest popular violent cartoon, for instance, youngsters don't learn how to engage their world. By engaging the industry-generated world instead, no self-determination is necessary. Little or no self-awareness results. Generative play, by contrast, continually requires the child to initiate an activity. The child learns to become proficient in making choices, having preferences, and experiencing consequences. With that comes self-awareness in a range of diverse situations.

The Power of Media Images

The power of visual media images lie in the emotions they arouse. Why do kids imitate images of anti-social behaviors so readily? At the end of the Power Rangers program, several of the Rangers would speak directly to the young audience saying, "Now remember, don't do these moves at home. Rather, be kind and treat your friends nicely." Do most youngsters follow this sound advice? No, of course not. The external image of the actual actions made much more of an impression than anything that was said afterwards.

Reproductive Play	Generative Play
Behavior imitates external images	New behaviors emerge as child filters external images from lots of experiences and uniquely combines them
Replicates TV Scripts	Invents own dialogue, makes up new words, employs poetic language
Only industry-generated toys	Empty boxes, kitchen utensils, junk mail, etc., whatever is available
Toys stay the same	Toys take on magical properties and become various things as child pretends
Uses memory to reproduce what is seen on TV to imitate what is seen on TV	Uses images from TV, books, life experiences to weave an original, creative play experience

Image making is clearly linked to emotional centers in our brains. Seeing pictures triggers emotional reactions. The more emotionally laden the image, the more the image will be replayed and remembered. Images of sex or violence arouse strong emotions, even causing physiological reactions. When the human brain takes in an image it doesn't easily go away. That is, the greater the emotional reaction felt upon viewing the image, the longer it stays. Images, therefore, are extremely powerful because, unlike words, they are not easily forgotten.

That's why it's so critical that the images that surround kids reflect a positive human model. With a lot of negative media images, the child absorbs negative emotions. In my book on media violence, *Stop Teaching Our Kids to Kill*, I point out that an important concern with media violence is that kids come to identify with the perpetrators of the violence and not with the victims. If children and teens were exposed to screen violence and empathized with the victims of the violence, they would be less likely to be imitating the violent behavior they see on TV, movies, or video games. Feeling the feelings of the victims would induce empathy. And it does in some children. But what the perpetrator does is more emotionally-laden, inducing hormonal and physiological reactions. Therefore, it's much easier to receive the perpetrator's message. The stronger the emotions induced, the more vivid the image. There is no way to avoid that—it's how the human brain functions. Paying more attention, then, to the perpetrator, is a natural consequence of the brain's operating system that will focus on the most salient, disturbing, arousing images. In addition, the perpetrator usually appears to be more powerful than the victim. For a child just beginning to learn about personal power, it's safer to identify with the powerful than it is with the weak. Where does that leave us then? With children's heads filled with images of murder and sadism. With their self-identities shaped by such images. Even if the research wasn't clear on the correlation between watching violence and becoming more violent, why would society want to fill its children's minds with such horrible images?

Walking through an airport during one Halloween weekend I saw a child that was turned toward a television screen showing ordinary people changing into vicious monsters. The little girl, about three years old, watched, becoming frightened. Her father was not turned toward the TV and had no idea what she had just seen. She started crying and he had no idea why. If she had nightmares that could easily result from exposure to such images, he would be left baffled why his daughter was so upset. She can't easily tell him, and he doesn't have enough information to ask her any questions.

Dr. Joanne Cantor, a communications professor at the University of Wisconsin-Madison, has done extensive research on fright reactions to scary TV and movie images. Transformation imagery, where a person changes into a malevolent character, can be particularly troublesome. Young children learn to trust that their parents are who they are and won't become somebody else. This is known as "person identity" and is a learned understanding that helps the child trust his or her world. Dr. Cantor explains, "in one famous study, children between the ages of three and six were allowed to pet a tame and friendly cat, and then watched its hindquarters while a researcher placed a realistic mask of a vicious dog over the cat's face. Although the animal had never been out of their sight, many of the younger children believed that when the animal turned around, it had become a dog...these children showed more fear in the presence of this 'new' animal than their older counterparts, who understood that the new appearance did not change who the animal was or whether it could hurt them. This study illustrates that little by little, children come to understand certain fundamental rules of the physical world. One of these is that people and animals have underlying identities that are not affected by momentary changes in their appearance."[17]

Preschoolers, like the little girl in the airport, get confused about transformations they see on screens. Just as the children in the study did not grasp that kittens were not dogs, the little girl likely did not understand how people can change into monsters. Around the age of four or five, youngsters come to trust person identity. But scary images still impact them powerfully. As Cantor explains, "So imagine that you're a child who has mastered this reassuring concept [of person identity] and you're watching television. There's a story about a very nice-looking man, kind, and thoughtful man. Suddenly this character you've come to like and trust starts to grow very fast, turns green, and becomes a grotesque monster before your eyes—this is scary. Maybe a physical transformation like this suddenly calls into question a lot of the reassuring principles you have come to rely on. If their man can suddenly change in this way, maybe other people can, too."[18] I have talked with parents who took their young children to see the 2003 movie, *The Incredible Hulk*, not understanding the impact it would have on them. Many had to leave the theater because their children were too anxious and afraid to watch the movie. We have to be very careful of exposing young children to images that they can't handle. Too many parents are taking their youngsters, even their infants, to ultra-violent movies and thinking nothing of it. Perhaps these types of practices will halt when more parents truly understand the power of visual imagery to induce corresponding emotions.

The Power of Human Image Making

While we can't erase a horrific image once it enters a child's mind, we can understand that internally-generated images and positive external images are as powerful as negative ones. With all the horrific visual violence on mass display and with only bad news getting airplay, it may seem counterintuitive to say that humans will orient toward positive images and really want to feel positive emotions since that doesn't seem like what is happening. But there is a body of scholarly research to indicate that people will "evolve in the direction of positive anticipatory images of the future."[19] Just like cats who seek a spot of sunshine for a nap or plants that turn toward the light, humans seek the positive. How do we reconcile this fact with the fact that negative images attract millions? First, I think we must make a distinction between being fascinated and being fed. Negative, horrific, and sensational images fascinate us. But they don't feed our souls. Rather, they intrigue us and keep us constricted within our low brain sensibilities. Positive images, on the other hand, nourish our highest aspirations and make it possible to live more fully. They appeal to the human neo-cortex, the place in the brain where our humanity is most fully developed.

Secondly, once children receive a steady diet of negative images, they come to identify with them. They naturally hold onto them. With masses of children and teens fed a steady diet of negative images daily for eighteen impressionable years, more people become adults who choose negative images by default. Start replacing these negative images with positive ones in early childhood and they will start growing to choose positive images that evoke positive emotions. Turning our attention away from industry-generated mania and towards the natural world can help a lot. Environmentalist Thomas Berry has written, "If we have powers of imagination, these are activated by the magic display of color and sound, of form and movement, such as we observe in the clouds of the sky, the trees and bushes and flowers, the waters and the wind, the singing birds, and the movement of the great whale through the sea. If we lived on the moon, our mind and emotions, our speech, our imagination…would all reflect the desolation of the lunar landscape."[20] The industry-generated culture, in effect, offers our kids a desolate landscape from which to derive their internal images. We can replace those by helping children value and use their own image-making capacities.

Image Making and the Parenting Process

The camera zooms toward the face of the young gymnast, who, with eyes closed, is bobbing her head this way, then that. Up and down, back and forth, she replays her next moves in her mind as she is about to mount the parallel bars at the Summer Olympics.

Coming home from her first college basketball practice, a young woman opens the folder of information that her coach gave everyone. She leafs through the pages. What's this? "Visualization Exercises for Enhanced Performance?"

A sixth grade boy at baseball camp enters a meeting late and hears his coach say, "See yourself hitting a home run in your mind's eye."

From well-trained athletes to middle schoolers, imagery techniques have gained in popularity. This mind-body connection used to seem far-fetched, but even reputable cancer centers and various clinics and hospitals employ professionals who teach methods for holding an image of optimal health in order to gain more optimal health. In our daily lives, image making is still not something most people pay much attention to. For instance, when I first suggest to concerned parents that changing the mental picture of their child will also change parenting practices, they seem a bit

To Help Develop Young Children's Image Making Capacities

"Wow! Your drawing shows you paid attention to the pictures in your head."

"Before I read another page in the book, let's talk for a few minutes about any pictures you are seeing in your head."

"Is what you see in your head the same as this picture in the book? Describe for me what you see in your head."

"Your brain certainly knows how to be imaginative. Look at the puzzle you put together (the art project you finished, the puppet play you did, etc.)."

"Yes, that was a good movie. But I want you to know: You can make up creative images in your head, too, just as good, or better than the ones we just saw."

"We will read one book about cats with pictures and another book about cats without pictures. Then you can draw your own pictures of cats, OK?"

bewildered. But research indicates that if we did that in any area of our lives—athletics, health, or parenting, we could increase our effectiveness, along with our energy.

Schools, for instance, are beginning to be more vocal about the power of visual imagery. "If we are honest about the cultures of most schools and most school systems, they downplay imagination, particularly among adults," Hayes Mizell told the Middle School Leadership Team of the Corpus Christi

Independent School District recently. In fact, Mizell said that "many educators constantly seek more specific direction so they will not have to use their imaginations. They want principals, central office and state department of education staff, and policy makers to tell them exactly what to do, perhaps because they want others to be accountable for results, or lack of them." Mizell reminded the audience that "only when educators imagine how their students can learn and perform at higher levels, and only when educators imagine how they can change their practice to achieve that result, is there hope for learning that energizes both teachers and students."[21]

You may have heard about something called the Pygmalion Effect. In the first study of this kind teachers were led, on the basis of expert opinion, to hold a positive image or expectancy of some students and a negative one of other students. Unknown to the teachers, the so-called high expectancy students were chosen at random. Then as the experiment progressed the researchers found that "differences quickly emerged, not on the basis of any innate intelligence factor or some other predisposition but solely on the basis of the manipulated expectancy of the teacher. Over time subtle changes among students evolve into clear differences as the high positive image students begin to significantly overshadow all the others in actual achievement."[22] This study has been replicated many times. In fact, over the last twenty years, there have been over 300 studies that clearly demonstrate the remarkable power of positive image and expectation on students' classroom performance.[23] As David Cooperrider, a leading thinker and writer on the effect of positive images states, "This shows us how essentially modifiable the human self is in relation to the mental projections of others…we are each made and imagined in the eyes of one another."[24]

Some of the images we hold, though, aren't positive ones. Anxiety and fear can sweep over us parents at any time of the day or night. When my sons were little boys, I worried that they wouldn't do well in school or would have tough times making friends. Other fleeting images would terrify me: they would wander off the playground and never be seen again, someone would kidnap them as they got off the school bus. As they grew, my "Inner Mommy Images" became more sophisticated in the fear they could engender in me. It's a frightening world and our mental models sometimes reflect it.

Parenting from a place of fear isn't fun or really very productive. What I see in truly understanding the power of our image-making capacities is that we can change our inner picture whenever we choose. This can bring a semblance of reassurance during parental anxiety attacks. "OK," we can say to a fearful image, "of course you are there because I naturally worry as a parent, but let's see another, more hopeful image right now." And just as quickly as pushing the button on our remotes, we can see in our mind's eye good things happening for and to our kids. What a relief! As we spend more time consciously changing our inner pictures about our kids, we relax more. Moreover, we are more likely to base our parental decisions on what is really happening rather than on imagined fears.

Image making can also get us through the trials of a difficult developmental stage. When we are having a particularly hard morning with an active toddler, for instance, we can imagine her as an energetic lawyer going the distance for her clients or as a curious scientist making an important breakthrough. With such a mental picture, we may come up with a way to frame a response or direct an action that keeps us centered. Thinking of a lively toddler as a bull-dog lawyer, instead of losing our temper over her stubbornness, we may comment, "You sure are holding to your beliefs right now." Then thinking of her as a curious scientist may give us an idea that saves the morning: "Here, I know you are curious about Mommy's bracelet. I'll let you look at it once we get your shirt on."

Positive images can spur parental breakthroughs. Tapping into our image making abilities goes a long way to reduce anxiety and stress, as well. And what is equally attractive about actively using our image-making is that we get more in touch with the big picture during the small things we do every day. Take for instance the example above: Helping a fussy toddler get dressed in the morning when you are crunched for time. What are most of us parents thinking at the time? (Be honest!) The average, busy parent is probably thinking a version of something like: "Come on, why does this have to be so difficult? Why do you have to pick this time to act up? I don't know what I'm going to do with her. Look at her at eighteen months, what will be like when she is two if she is so stubborn now?"

What most parents in such a scenario aren't saying to themselves is something like this: "When I help my youngster get dressed and give her alternatives and stay calm, I am modeling for her a way to make decisions. When I am patient and available to really listen to her, she will feel secure and loved."

Of course, we aren't thinking that. We are only human. When under stress, it's hard to remember what we are parents for. This is where using our image making can help. We naturally pay attention to what we need to pay attention to. Thus, in the midst of a vexing struggle with a child, it takes work to imagine something different. But when we see our child in the future with the skills, talents, and a personality we are trying to nurture, it redirects us. It can even make us laugh; or gently remind us of the absurdity of the moment. As adults, our inner image making capacity allows us to re-create our response to what is happening in our environment. It can literally take us out of an annoying present reality and dump us into a new reality.

Parents can have a profound effect on their children by holding a positive expectancy image of their son or daughter. This doesn't mean to "push" our children or mold them into something they are not. On the contrary, by keeping an image alive in our minds that focuses on our kids' full human potential, we relax more. We can allow our children to blossom at their own pace because we are less likely to panic that our kids are not measuring up in some way. With positive images we are less likely to worry or be in states of anxiety about our kids when they encounter life's inevitable struggles. This not only brings us hope as parents, it also conveys a can-do attitude to our children. We show them that we believe in them, and in turn, they come to believe in themselves.

By keeping an image in our minds of our children as capable and creative, for instance, we also change the way we practice parenting. Like a teacher who comes to see a student in a different light and thereby adapts a teaching method to align with this "new image" of the student, so too do parents employ different ways to discipline or to communicate with their children when their internal image of them changes. Let's look at what occurred with Kay and her fifteen year-old daughter Julie. When Julie was fourteen, Kay realized that Julie's running off to the bathroom after meals was not a "little indigestion" as Julie had told her. Rather, Julie was suffering from bulimia. That was indeed creating digestive and other serious health problems for her. Kay was beside herself with worry. She told me, "When I look at Julie I see this desperate, fragile child who just can't cope with life." I suggested to Kay, "Try seeing Julie in your mind's eye as healthy, vibrant, and able to cope with anything that comes her way. Think of Julie that way and observe how your interactions with her change." At first this was really hard for Kay to do. But over time she practiced and replaced negative inner images of Julie with positive ones. Since positive actions derive from positive images, Kay noticed how more gently she treated her daughter. When Julie came back from seeing her counselor, for instance, she didn't push to find out everything that went on. She became overall more trusting of Julie's healing process. One day after Julie was in therapy for six months, she came up to Kay and put her arms around her, "You know what I told Beth (her therapist) today? I told her that the way I am getting through all this is because of you believing in me so much."

Seeing such success, Kay went a step further. She talked with Julie about the power of positive mental imagery and suggested she hold an inner picture of her body as healthy. Together they looked at the slim female bodies in current magazines, discussing how these were unrealistic portrayals. Julie acknowledged that these were the images that were in her head. They were her ideal. Kay took out some photos of Julie at a younger age before her bulimia started. Julie was able to see her vitality, happiness, and health oozing from these pictures. It wasn't long until Julie told Kay that she was beginning to see a different internal image of herself—one that was healthier, with firmer, larger muscles. She surprised even herself when she realized that this was actually a more beautiful body than the skinny, lifeless one she was wanting. Julie began to take actions based on the new image of herself she now held. Over time the girl regained her health, along with her self-respect and a sense of peace about her body image.

An internal image acts like the North Star, guiding us and keeping us on course for what it is we wish to attain. While the consequences of visualization can seem miraculous, there is nothing hocus pocus about it. It's grounded in how human brains act. They are future-oriented. Like a movie-projector, they project the reality that we move toward. As we move toward that inner reality, we take actions that align with it. Our external reality then complies.

Discovering What the Inner Pictures Look Like

Our children can see negative images and interpret them in different ways. One young teen may see the negative image of a thin model and think, "How sad," while another, like Julie, might think, "That's for me." So one important practice as parents in a media age is to find out what images our kids do have in their heads. Kay made a breakthrough when she realized Julie's image of an attractive woman was a "starved" model. We can ask questions that help children and teens articulate more fully the images they are holding and then help them morph any negative images into positive ones. This can be a useful strategy as soon as a child has enough of a vocabulary to start speaking about what they see on screen technologies.

Some questions to ask younger children:

- Tell Mommy/Daddy what you remember from the movie.
- What was the best part for you?
- Let's talk about the beginning, the middle, and the end of the movie (cartoon, TV show). You draw a picture of the beginning, the middle, and/or the end. Then let's talk about it.
- When you (jump like that, kick like that, etc.) are you remembering where you first saw that action move?
- When you close your eyes, what picture do you see of the movie (cartoon, TV show)?

Some questions to ask older children and teens:

- After you watched that movie what are a few of the images you came away with?
- How do you picture that (movie, TV show) to yourself?
- When you play that video game, what types of images do you think about afterwards?
- Who in the movie would you most like to be like? Why?
- Before we watch, tell me what is your image of what this (movie, TV show) will be about? Afterwards let's talk about how it measured up to your image of it.

Another helpful strategy is to help kids link to the feelings of images they hold in their heads. For instance, your son is excited about coming in first place in the school's Science Fair. As you celebrate this success, you can ask: As you see yourself accepting the award, how does that make you feel?" Responses such as "Great," "Cool," "Happy," "Proud" help him associate positive feelings

To Help Older Kids Value Their Image Making Abilities

"Did the movie portray the book the way you thought? If you were making the book into a film, what would your images be?

"You can picture in your head whatever you choose to."

"Before we go on the picnic, (watch this video, take the boat ride, etc.) I'd like you to describe what image you have of what it might be like."

"Can you imagine a different alternative from what you just described?"

"I can see how you used your image making abilities to come up with this beautiful artwork (inventive science project, elegant solution, etc.)."

"Your imagination is powerful. Keep using it!"

with a positive image. When he experiences another positive internal picture, he will be more likely to feel the positive emotions with more self-awareness. As we talk with our children about the positive images they do see in the media, we can also amplify the positive feelings such images brought up. "Watching that documentary gave me a lot of hope. Those images of the people building houses for the homeless were very inspiring." By saying such a statement, your child will more likely walk away from the program focusing on positive images and feeling a sense of hope.

Using Our Image Making Abilities for Energized Parenting

With our image making capacities, we can learn to enter into longer and longer periods of positive realities. In working with parents at the Parent Coaching Institute, we use a process called Appreciative Inquiry to help with this. Appreciative Inquiry began with the work of David Cooperrider and his colleagues in the world of business. It applies so well to parenting because it shines a spotlight on our dream or vision—what we truly desire to live most fully. The first step is to get as clear as we can about our dream, or "preferred future." Then we keep as much as we can of the dream image in our heads. When that happens, we start feeling the excitement and hope that the dream image brings. This builds our energy. We naturally pay more attention to our dream because it now feels more attainable "Hmm…maybe this *is* possible," we say to ourselves, because the inner image has prompted never before considered real-world possibilities. The dream image fuels our desire. We then more easily make parenting choices based on our dream for ourselves and our children. As we hold dream images, they affect our actions.

We can also hold a dream for ourselves as well as our children. Many parents find this an enjoyable process that brings delightful surprises. Perhaps they want to be more patient or be better able to set firmer boundaries. Perhaps they want to be gentler on themselves and learn to appreciate themselves more for all they are doing for their children. By using our image making capabilities we can picture ourselves with the characteristics we'd like. We can see ourselves doing things differently. As we go through the process of dream-imaging and dream-building, we can share it in family meetings with our kids, and encourage them to try it for themselves.

We can also lead a family visioning process. This could mean imaging how we would like the upcoming week to look like or what joint goals are at this time. Whatever is bogging us down as a family can be re-constructed into a positive vision.

Regular family visioning processes hold many benefits. Research has shown that groups of people in close association with each other, like a family or a company, share common mental images about the group as a collaborative unit. Depending on the predominate language used, groups can share positive or negative mental images. These shared mental images are referred to as a group's "inner dialogue."[25] Just as individuals use self-talk, so do groups. A group's inner dialogue can spur aliveness or deaden it. For instance, when individuals in a group speak negatively using a vocabulary of despair, the mental images of everyone tend to be more negative. This results in a negative inner dialogue for everyone. Visioning processes, on the other hand, help keep the dialogue between family members upbeat. With hopeful vocabulary, everyone thinks and talks more positively. Research reports have indicated that "many of our children today are growing up in family settings where as much as ninety percent of the home's internal dialogue is negative, that is, what not to do, how bad things are, what was done wrong, who is to blame."[26] Your commitment to family visioning keeps everyone's mental images positive and your family's inner dialogue hopeful.

The overall outcome of positive image making is the gift of increased energy. Remember, we move in the direction of the images we hold most often. Let's keep them hopeful images. By parenting from such images, we not only increase our own sense of aliveness but our children's and family's as well.

To Nurture Your Image Making Abilities

Try a few of these exercises and observe which ones work best for you.

- Talk with your spouse or a friend about something you want, a special dream. Have the person ask you questions so that the dream is elaborated and as clear as it can be. Get in touch with the wonderful feelings of the dream and share them often with this person. Observe any changes in yourself and changes that occur in your life.

- Pay closer attention to a reoccurring mental image. Is it a daydream to soothe you? Does it induce anxiety or fear? What needs to change about this mental picture to bring you more ease and peace? Refine the image until it's exactly as you want it.

- Before a potentially contentious time with your child such as going out for an evening and leaving your son with a baby-sitter, or confronting your daughter about her poor grades on her report card, replay how you would like the conversation to go before it takes place. See in your mind's eye how you will handle the situation as clearly as you can. Imagine your child's reactions as you want them to be. After the actual conversation observe how the image-making before-hand helped.

- Find pictures in magazines that reflect a dream or a goal. Look at them as often as you can for a week. The next week, don't look at them at all. Instead use your mental imagery to picture what you want. Alternate weeks like this until your mental imagery matches the magazine pictures and you don't need them anymore.

6

The Fourth Essential Need: Creative Expression

Creative people. . .believe that there is something meaningful to accomplish each day, and they can't wait to get started on it.

Mihaly Csikszentmihalyi[1]

Have you ever had an experience like this?

You have completed a day, or week-long seminar, that's been extremely motivating. It spruced up your attitude and gave you lots of inspiration. Toward the end of it, though, something happened to dampen your spirit. You were required to write a poem, or tell an original story, or do something creative to share with the rest of the group. You panicked, thinking, "What could I do that would be creative enough?" As others did their presentations, you thought to yourself, "Mine isn't going to measure up. Look how creative all the others are. Mine is going to be stupid." Then when your turn came, something seemed to come over you. Maybe you found a stronger voice than you thought you had or you spontaneously changed something mid-stream as a new idea emerged "out of the blue." Whatever happened, it surprised and delighted you. After you finished, the others thanked you and seemed genuinely touched by your presentation. With your spirit back in high-gear, you left the workshop in awe, simultaneously appreciating the unexpected gift but still wondering where it came from.

It seems like this is a common experience for a lot of people. First, we worry and compare our creativity to others. That can make us feel inadequate. Then, when we take a risk and create something, it may still feel scary, but we dive in anyway. Once we are in the creative process, we find ideas that pleasantly surprise us, discovering more about our innate abilities. The process is usually humbling. We have to admit to ourselves that it seemed like another force, something else took hold of us and graced us, since the ideas came in so suddenly.

Welcome to the human process of creative expression. Creating puts us in touch with our very human fears and vulnerabilities. At the same time, it gives us access to the Divine in a special way. In a very real sense, the mark of being human is to co-create with a Higher Power. Writing in her book *The Lives of the Muses*, Francine Prose gives us a good reminder: "To create anything is to undergo the humbling and strange experience— like a mystical visitation or spirit possession—of making something and not knowing where it comes from. It's as if the magician had no idea how the rabbit got into his hat."[2] In the creative process, we get help from another Source. We never go at it alone. Creativity allows us to be fully human, bringing more spiritual good into the world. Unfortunately, too many people hold back their creative expression. They dismiss how important their authentic creativity is to their own well-being and to everyone they touch. If we keep focused on how uncomfortable it is to take a risk or on comparing ourselves with others, we can feel increasingly inadequate. We can forget that our unique talents and skills are great blessings—gifts that demand expression for the good of all.

Matthew Fox, who has written extensively on creativity, explains that "the etymological origin for the word 'hell' is *helan*, an old English word that means 'to conceal'...In other words, hell is our place of concealment. Hell, then, is our refusal to create and our deadening the imagination of others...the alternative to creativity is worse than death. It is boredom. A death of the Spirit. A soul-death...But if hell is concealment, then heaven must be creativity itself." [3]

In our industry-generated culture, many people are bored and depressed, seeking a sense of aliveness through drugs, sex, or shopping, instead of through their own creativity. Hiding out in addictions means we don't ever have to grow up and become responsible creators. That would take some bravery. As poet e. e. cummings wrote, "It takes courage to grow up and turn out to be who you really are." [4] But the larger culture promotes dissatisfaction with life as it is, so it may even take more than courage to be who we are. It may take a true understanding of our human nature along with deep respect for our need to create. If we really thought of creative expression as an important human need, we all probably would do more of it. Since the industry-generated culture keeps most people turned toward superficialities that never bring satisfaction, the unsane habit of concealing one's authentic creative expression becomes more "the norm" in our society than the normal human need to create. Sam Keen, author of several insightful books, including *The Passionate Life*, has observed that "the epidemic of boredom and depression is a symptom of cultural rather than individual failure." [5] When we live in a culture that doesn't support our full human potential, many people will stay bored and depressed.

The industry-generated culture hooks us into the idea that individual, small creative endeavors aren't as important as mass displays of creative output. Believing this, it becomes safer not attempting anything that might nudge our creativity to fuller maturity. After all, we could go crazy comparing ourselves with creative musicians who write fantastic scores for movies or with immensely talented photographers whose photos we see as we leaf through magazines in the dentist's office. With all the showy stuff constantly around us, refuge in passive entertainment means no one laughing at or scorning our seemingly awkward expressions. But at what cost to us as individuals, as families, and as society? Concealing our own truths, we buy into false realities, stifling our imaginative spirits. Others, including our children, are short-changed whenever we hold back our creative expressions. When millions of families watch someone else's creative expressions on television five or six hours every night, they bring less good into the world. It's interesting and ironic to note that Madonna reportedly doesn't let her kids watch television and I've heard that Arnold Schwarzeneger and Maria Shriver don't allow their children to watch TV during school nights. Creative parents, even those who work in the industry, know screen machines can dampen creative expression. But in far too many families, living rooms become less about living and more about death of our collective spirit. And the children notice.

Somehow, too many U. S. adults have forgotten about the human need to create beyond the work world. As more prisons get built, as more children take to the streets, as our society's infrastructure crumbles around us, everyone of us has a responsibility to take our creative expression more seriously. Who knows what good we could collectively unleash if each of us followed through on only a fraction of the creative ideas that come to us?

This chapter is about enhancing our own creative expression as well as our children's. It examines how human creativity gets stifled in an industry-generated culture and what to do about it. We look at making room for the psychic space and the physical space needed for the components of creativity in our everyday lives. Finally, we explore parenting itself as an art form that can unleash exciting new ways of being with our children and ourselves.

Creative Expression in an Industry-Generated Culture

We all know the joy of finishing a project, whether it's writing a research paper, knitting a sweater, or painting a room in our home. Accomplishment renews us and propels us to continue to create. In so doing, we feel better and make our life a little bit better at the same time. Some would say that this type of creative expression is creativity with a small "c." And that the other type of creative expression, such as the works of van Gogh, for instance, is creative expression with a capital "C." But big "C" creativity is often a matter of preference, opinion, or social acceptance. Walking through the Museum of Modern Art in New York City, my sister, an accomplished watercolor artist, could hardly believe some of the paintings that "passed for art." One in particular, a small black dot on the middle of a white background, caught our attention. I had to agree with her—we were both making such "masterpieces" in first grade. After admiring the Monet which covered a large wall with breathtaking colors, there seemed no comparison.

While what's termed "creative" may be subjective, it's the act of the creative process itself that is so human. We were born to create. In an industry-generated culture, many parents lead such busy lives that rather than being in a creative process, they are in a reactive one. Not making up new forms or new ways, they find solace in well-worn answers, rather than develop new solutions. But many very much appreciate being nudged to consider thinking creatively. For instance, when I suggest to parents that they approach home screens in a creative way, such as putting a blanket over the TV and listening to a program once in a while or showing the children a travel video of a national park while pretending to be there, they easily come up with other creative ways for family viewing. Screen machine interactions don't have to be passive. But, as a society, we are so caught up in how things are, we aren't creating new, exciting ways to be with screen technologies. It's as if, in an industry-generated culture, parental creative expression in regard to home screens is on a sabbatical.

Although we are a country of tremendous creativity and productivity on many fronts, commonplace creativity, as I call it, seems to be getting rarer. Commonplace creativity consists of small, daily creative acts that bring parents and children a sense of aliveness and connection to life and to each other. Laughing together as we "watch" a TV with a blanket over it is one such example. Personal hobbies are good examples, too. But outside of computers or video games, few children these days have hobbies like stamp collecting, crafts, or sewing. One summer while driving through Vancouver, British Columbia on a beautiful spring afternoon, I spotted a girl about ten years old sketching under a tree in a public park. I was taken by this image because I had never encountered a child with a sketch pad in a park in the United States. Are kids here so tethered to screen machines, they can't think of anything else to do with their time? Art, dance, and other forms of creative expression are the first to go with budget cuts in public schools caught up in a mechanistic mind-set that pours money into testing programs for rote-learning while ignoring such creative expressions. Yet, these commonplace forms of creativity are so critical to help kids engage fully with life and develop their unique talents and skills. Too many children are growing up with adult role models demonstrating to them that their creativity is of little or no importance.

This is truly tragic. As some humans increasingly create destructive forces such as smarter bombs or improved artillery, it's important that our children don't lose touch with their commonplace, constructive creativity. The hallmark of being human is constructive, rather than destructive, creativity. When a person knits a beautiful sweater, they usually don't pull it apart or cut it to shreds with scissors. A person who paints a wall to beautify a room, doesn't usually willingly dirty it to mar the effect. These behaviors would be considered deviant. It seems much more of a human longing and built-in human tendency to create constructively. But when do children get such an opportunity? If their leisure time is filled up in front of screen machines, what are they actually creating? With passive television, there is nothing generated by the child. No decision to be made. No problem to be solved. Nothing to show for the time in front of a program except that time has passed, the child is a little bit older. The child, then, does not know herself or himself as a creator. Caught up in passive entertainment, the child's self-identity is distanced from the know-how, the conviction, and the will required for submersion in a creative process. While passive television can give the creative person impetus and ideas for something new, a child who is not in touch with his or her own creativity can't find inspiration or personal meaning in front of a screen machine. It's not a catalyst for creative expression, but a crutch to avoid it all together. Not learning to swim with ease in the waters of creativity, children habituated to passive TV flail and thrash about when expected to generate new ideas. They don't trust that their own creative process will hold them afloat during the challenging times inherent in any creative act. Instead, they distrust their creative capacities simply because they have not had enough experiences using them.

The industry-generated culture gains mindless consumers when kids don't identify themselves as creators. Being a passive receiver of industry-generated messages means kids can come to believe the greatest con of this culture: What sells is what is of most value. Creating something beautiful that doesn't have a price on it is outside this culture's purview. Commerce, not art, education, or the common people's opinions, is held in highest regard. Creativity is evaluated on how many copies were sold. Blurring the distinction between art and product, a lot of kids grow up thinking their creative expression worthless. Since they can't sell it to the masses, what good it is? When children get this message continually from little on up, they can come to de-value themselves, along with their creativity. This can lead to feelings of frustration and disconnection to others which can lead to a gamut of destructive and self-destructive feelings and behaviors. Constructive creativity, on the other hand, helps develop confidence, self-appreciation, and a connection to life.

So, the first step for parents in meeting this essential need is to help children value their creative expression. Valuing themselves as creators means children will probably use commonplace constructive creativity as a natural part of their daily lives. Also, they are more likely to grow up with a healthy perspective of the current industry-generated culture and a positive attitude about changing what is not working. They will be able to think beyond what is presently available and be able to generate something better.

Encouraging kids to value themselves as creators can be done intentionally throughout a busy day. Here are some examples of encouraging statements you can make for children of different ages. I'm sure you'll think of others that are best-suited for your child.

Encouraging statements for young children
- You can be pleased with your drawing. You put a lot of good ideas into it.
- I know you can do that!
- You seem frustrated right now, but I want you to try again after you feel better.
- Remember when you thought you couldn't do
  _____, but you did? You are a wonderful creator, never forget that.
- I value your creative abilities.

Encouraging statements for older children

- I like that idea. It really shows you are using your creativity.
- It's important that you appreciate your creative abilities. Take some time tonight to think about all the wonderful things you have created recently. Then let's talk about how you can tackle this project.
- I love seeing you taking your creativity seriously.
- I know you don't feel like _____ right now. But I bet you can think of a creative way to approach this.
- I encourage you to think how your creativity can help you here.

Encouraging statements for teens

- The time you spent on _____ really shows you value your creativity.
- You are looking at this situation in a fresh light. Aren't you proud of how you can see different alternatives?
- I value your creative ideas. They always add to our family discussions.
- Your creativity will serve you well in your career choice.
- Creative expression in _____ seems to suit you.
- I can see that you are valuing your creative ideas. That's good, because they're great!

Another way to help children and teens value their creative expression is to encourage these four components of creativity:

- Fluency
- Flexibility
- Originality
- Elaboration

These major attributes, researched by E. Paul Torrance and his associates, were found to be present in people who used their creativity often.[6] When kids use them, they come to value their creative expression more because they experience it being present and available in their daily routines.

Fluency

Fluency is the ability to come up with a lot of ideas in a short amount of time. Brainstorming is a great technique you can use to help kids tap into their fluency abilities. At family meetings, for instance, brainstorming can be used to figure out how to delegate the household chores, how to get homework accomplished more easily, or decide where to go on a family vacation. Kids of all ages enjoy blurting out ideas as parents record them on a large poster paper or on a whiteboard. There is no holding back and no judgment of the ideas thrown out. The important thing is to have fun and affirm everyone's ideas.

Once there is a pool of ideas to choose from, kids and parents can take time discussing the various options and giving their opinions. This activity further hones children's creative expression because now they have to articulate reasons for choices and get in touch with their priorities as they acknowledge others' opinions, too. With a few family brainstorming sessions like this, parents can encourage both children and teens to use the technique when they want to figure out what to do, but aren't quite sure how. Deciding how to talk to a friend about something potentially upsetting or how to approach a coach about getting more playing time are ways kids can use brainstorming to help clarify what their next steps might be. In addition, when kids face dilemmas, parents can ask a question like, "What are other ideas you can think of?" or give a reassurance like, "Let's see if we can think of a few more options together," which will further kids' fluency skills. Try them when children may be frustrated and on the verge of whining. It's a great feeling to know that when you put your mind to it, more ideas will appear.

Flexibility

Flexibility is characterized by the ability to see various perspectives and not hold on rigidly to certain ways of doing things. Creative people usually exhibit a remarkable capacity for flexibility. If one way isn't working, they try something different. They aren't afraid to experiment, run a risk, or fail. Flexibility can be encouraged by noticing and affirming when our children let go and look in a fresh direction. For instance, when a child acquiesces and no longer pushes to go to the restaurant of her choice, you can say, "You are being so flexible. I appreciate your willingness to try something different." Or when your child lets a sibling have his way, "That was really flexible of you. Being flexible is a great attribute to have because you'll be able to get along with a lot of people."

Parents can also encourage flexibility in children's creative endeavors. When a child complains about not liking the picture he drew, you can point out ways he or she can add something else to it to make it into a different picture. You can remind your child that many great artists had similar experiences. Some even made it a regular routine to paint over pictures with new ideas. Imaginative play, also, is a great teacher of flexibility. Sherry Turkle, professor at MIT, emphasizes that in imaginative play, "children have to learn to put themselves in the place of another person, to imagine what is going on inside someone else's head." [7]

Another way to help kids to see other perspectives is to use "What If" inquiries. Some fun questions:

- If you explained your homework assignment to someone from a different country, how would you say it?
- If you were the morning paper, what are you thinking as you are being read?
- If Napoleon and John Lennon held a conversation, what would they talk about?
- If birds couldn't fly, how would they travel?

You will notice that good flexibility questions begin with the word, "if." Point that out to your child. Now be prepared to stretch your flexibility muscles answering his or her "if" questions!

Originality

We can usually spot originality, but no specific definition works well because originality, like creativity itself, can be so subjective. Nevertheless, what we want to encourage in our youngsters are ways of thinking that reflect our kids' uniqueness. "Thinking out of the box," is a common way of saying "being original." With similar images being repeated continuously over televisions for hours daily, children can get the impression that replicating sameness is the way to go. Really, though, inventing uniqueness is what makes life more interesting and humans more interested in life. Many parents I know discover that introducing kids to all types of world music—from classical to jazz to folk—or various forms of poetry or different types of artwork provides them with important models for originality. We live in an immensely diverse world. But we usually have to go beyond the bounds of an industry-generated culture to access it.

Sometimes kids mimic industry-generated sameness and think they are being original. One mother I coached had a thirteen year-old daughter who started dressing provocatively, imitating overtly sexual female celebrities. Yet, the girl valued her individuality. Her artistic flare, instead of being innovative, was inappropriate. Eventually, this mother had success, though, helping her daughter express herself within a certain set of boundaries. They found great sweaters at consignment stores and sewed on flower decals. The girl enjoyed dying old blouses and skirts for a different, colorful look. As she took more control of her individual fashion, she realized that she was making more clothes choices based on her own creative expression and not on ideas dictated by media images. Her mother was relieved to be able to encourage the girl's authentic creativity. Joseph Chilton Pearce makes an important point when he writes that "anything is possible, but what is appropriate?"[8] As our kids express their uniqueness, they also have to learn what is appropriate and socially acceptable.

Elaboration

The final component of creativity is the ability to spend time elaborating, adding details and making sure the creative expression is as one intended. Many kids learn through fast-paced TV and video games that quick is better. This is not the case in most creative projects. Time and care must be taken to embellish and refine the new creation. Schools that teach the writing process give children the opportunity to practice this component of creativity when they polish their writing in the final stages. But a lot of kids want to race on to the next project once they have their basic ideas down. Parents can make sure their children slow down and sit with the finished product for awhile. This gives time to carefully consider what the children may wish to add before calling it finished. Encouraging kids to take their time and not rush through the writing process, or any project, develops children's attention to the importance of elaboration.

Detail-oriented people may find it easier to flesh out projects. Those of us who are more global in our viewpoint may need to work at it more. Consider pointing out to your child when he or she uses elaboration. For instance, if you notice your son commenting on every detail on the family's new car, you can let him know that his focus on such details can help him focus on others, such as the finer points of dribbling a basketball or the number of adjectives he uses when writing a descriptive paragraph.

Losing Self-Consciousness

In addition to helping children value their creative expression through the techniques discussed above, we can also support children's creative expression by helping them "lose themselves" in their creative process. For instance, when we are really "into" doing something we love, we often lose track of time and forget about ourselves in the process. You have probably experienced looking up at the clock while doing something enjoyable, startled to see how much time has passed by. By losing self-consciousness we gain more conscious awareness of what we are doing in the moment. Being fully present to each detail of the creative process we are in makes time fly. Some people call this being in the "zone" or in a "flow." Here is an example:

A twelve year-old boy in a seventh-grade language arts classroom was busy creating a children's book for preschoolers. His teacher noticed how engrossed he was in this creative act. He took his time selecting the right colors as he sketched an intricate design, aimed at getting little children "hooked." He pondered word selection. How can I say what I want to say so a three year-old can understand? He smiled delightedly to himself when an insight came to him. Abruptly, he looked up and announced to his teacher, "I forgot to take my meds today and I'm not even hyper!"

This was a startling revelation for the boy and a telling observation for teachers and parents. It prompted his teacher to ask me, "Could Jim get rid of his meds if he were more engaged in intellectually stimulating and creative activities and cut out television?" This is a question worth pondering. When kids are over stimulated, either by medications or by the perceptual chaos of screen machines, it becomes harder for them to concentrate. As their focus lessens, they get more easily distracted. A person who can get easily distracted has a very difficult time losing self-consciousness. They can't pour their attention into what they are doing because they are interrupted too frequently. With increased interruptions, they have to put more effort into their creative task. With too many disturbances, the process becomes a difficult burden, instead of something fun and easy to do. The child who can't concentrate can't "invest attention" into his or her own creative process. Research studies demonstrate that "instead of requiring more effort, investment of attention actually seemed to decrease mental effort."[9] In other words, the better people can concentrate, the less mental work required to complete the task.

Parents who help their children "invest attention" give them an extremely important gift. When children can concentrate, they have the necessary prerequisite to lose themselves in a creative act. They can then find the delight and personal power that comes with the feelings of creative accomplishment. Without the ability to concentrate, the child will have a much more difficult time experiencing "flow" or any ease when they want to create. A lot of kids gravitate toward TV or video games simply because they want to feel what this "flow" might be like. Staring at a television can bring on an alpha brain wave state, inducing feelings of relaxation. In fact, some studies indicate that our brains are more active when sleeping than when watching television.[10] This alpha state can be confused with a creative flow state. So, rather than being in a "zone," the kids are zoned out. Video games bring about a similar brain state. In her book *The Second Self,* Sherry Turkle writes, "When you play a video game you enter into the world of the programmers who made it. You have to do more than identify with a character on the screen. You must act for it. Identification through action has a special kind of hold...for many...what is pursued in the video game is not a score, but an altered state...the pace is never yours. The rhythm of the game belongs to the machine, the program decides."[11] Although there are video games that require kids to choose an adventure or continually make a decision, their choices are limited to what is offered by the game developer. When children enter their own creative process, however, they are not entering someone else's world. Rather, they invent something that is personally meaningful. The rhythm belongs to them. The pace is always theirs. The "altered state" they experience is a natural outcome of attention investment in creative expression and the feelings of delight and exhilaration that accompany it.

Here are several key strategies that will help kids of any age increase their abilities of concentration:

- Require your son or daughter to complete homework and/or a creative project before or instead of watching any television, going to a movie, or playing video games.

- Keep the television off whenever a child is playing in the room, doing homework, or working on any project that requires concentration. It's not only distracting, it will limit the child's capacity to actually develop concentration abilities.

- Don't allow children under the age of ten to play video games. Gameboys, in particular, can damage young children's attention spans. When your child has developed habits of mind that show you that he or she can experience long periods of time in creative expression (without screens), then you can allow some non-violent video game play. Consider such rules as: Video game playing only on weekends; for every video game played a concept for a new one has to be created by your child; when his or her friends come over, spend time doing a creative project instead of video game playing.

- Make a wide variety of creative projects available that would be fun for your child to do. Research shows that "people who enjoy themselves in a wide variety of situations have the ability to screen out stimulation and to focus on what they decide is relevant for the moment." [12]

Making Psychic Space for Creative Expression

In order to create consistently, we all need available energy. That energy comes from psychic space that we nurture through:
- Solitude
- Discovery
- Enjoyment of Complexity

Solitude

The previous two essential needs, an inner life and image making, discussed in Chapters Four and Five, build upon each other and provide psychic space for creative expression. With time inside of self a person refines his or her mind, developing a multi-faceted personality. With diverse interests and a well-tuned brain to engage new ideas, creative expression flows more easily. Mihaly Csikszentmihalyi, along with his colleagues at the University of Chicago, interviewed ninety-one highly creative, exceptional individuals These men and women included distinguished historians, composers, philosophers, poets, writers, visual artists, architects, psychologists, biologists, physicians, chemists, economists, and social activists. Most had been honored with prestigious awards; fourteen had won the Noble Prize. Among

Television Watching as a Creative Activity

What would happen if...

- Your family watched a favorite TV program together as if they were important critics, and then discussed it afterwards?

- Your family turned the sound off during a show and each person made up and shared his/her own interpretive dialogue about the action?

- Your family put a blanket over the television and everyone just listened and later discussed how it felt to make up your images of the action?

- Your child had to give two reasons for watching each program based on how it would enhance his or her creativity?

- During the commercials, you asked your children: What does it want me to think? What does it want me to feel?

- You asked your child to picture what was happening off-camera?

- You had your child communicate what happened on the program without using words?

- You muted the commercials and asked your child what will happen next?

- Your family watched educational stations more often than commercial ones?

the important findings in this study was that "the traits that distinguish a complex personality are likely to add a higher statistical probability of creative expression." [13]

It may seem too easy that loving our children, talking with them, helping them get in touch with their inner life, and supporting their image-making capacities would enable them to form complex personalities, capable of high levels of creativity. Call it the "great parental paradox": seemingly simple parental activities enable children's brains to develop high levels of complexity, and with that, capacities for creative expression. In some cases of the creative individuals studied, a parent died or the bonding was broken in some way. It seems that when the other two essential needs of developing an interior life and image making were met, their creativity wasn't shortchanged. If the individuals were able to make sense out of the early trauma, they could live very productive, creative lives. Having an inner life and imagination helped them do this and acted as buffers to emotional distress. [14]

Csikszentmihalyi found in his study that "children who have not learned to tolerate solitude are especially at risk in terms of never developing enough in-depth involvement in a domain, lacking opportunities to reflect and incubate ideas." [15] The first stage of any creative process is an incubation stage. Time to reflect and think is critical. You have probably noticed young children needing a lot of time to arrange play materials before they dive into the experience or just sitting and thinking for a few minutes before beginning.

Parents, too, need some time to sort out thoughts before beginning something new. This important "down time," discussed in Chapter Four, allows for creative ideas to bubble to the surface.

Without enough reflection time, we can't easily muster the psychic energy to pursue anything. We don't feel very alive, let alone creative. When we are under sustained stress this is especially true. One mother of seven-year-old twins, who had just gone through a divorce, told me that all summer she took her children to a beach, where they could play and she could just sit undisturbed. Everyday, without fail, they spent at least four to five hours this way. She explained, "When I was sitting on the sand, enjoying the sun, I tried reading books and magazines. But I couldn't get into them. All I wanted was peace with no demands. Even reading seemed too much. I just wanted to sit and do nothing. As the girls enjoyed playing on the beach, they didn't interrupt me as much as they would at home. I was surprised I was so hungry for this kind of down time. But by September I felt like a new woman. That month I tackled a new job, a move across town, and getting the girls settled into a new school. It was all fun and exciting to me. I doubt whether I would have had this kind of drive if I hadn't spent most of my summer staring into space."

Discovery

During his study of creative individuals Csikszentmihalyi found that "all too often the joy of discovery fails to be communicated to young people, who turn instead to passive entertainment. But consuming culture is never as rewarding as producing it. If it were only possible to transmit the excitement of the people we interviewed to the next generation, there is no doubt that creativity would flourish." [16]

Why has the excitement of discovery been extinguished for many children and teens? An industry-generated culture pushes a mind-set of pseudo-sophistication. To be "cool," kids can't express awe, joy, or authentic delight spontaneously. They have to hold back or their peers will think them "weird." Interview kids who have little exposure to television or who are home-schooled. They have less investment in industry-generated mythologies and it shows. Twelve year-olds still have some wide-eyed innocence. Fifteen year-olds enthusiastically share their plans or opinions. Their curiosity about lots of things—about life in general—spills forth. Their sense of wonder is intact.

One synonym for discovery in Roget's 21st Century Thesaurus is "to bring to light." Children and teens who enjoy discovery bring to light their skills and talents. Their minds become free to enjoy creative expression. With enjoyment comes even more inner space to receive insights and develop ideas. Encouraging our children's sense of wonder and curiosity—at any age—will lead them to have increased energy for creative expression and experience a continual enhancement of their creative abilities.

Enjoyment of Complexity

Healthy hearts beat regularly. Healthy lungs breathe easily. The human brain, given its natural state, thinks. It actually likes to think, even enjoying a certain amount of complexity. This doesn't mean parents should push kids or frustrate them with tasks that are too difficult. What it does mean, though, is that we must expect that our kids are capable of enjoying mental challenges. Yes, actually enjoying and even seeking mental effort! This may sound strange given the fact that too many kids today shy away from complex problems, or when faced with a challenging task, they often get frustrated and give up too soon. This is so commonplace as to seem normal. But it isn't.

In an industry-generated culture, kids are too stressed. Learning gets shortchanged when the human brain has to deal with stress on top of any mental effort. In fact, not seeking or enjoying complexity should be a major red flag to parents that the child or teen is under too much stress. When kids are appropriately challenged in an environment that minimizes stress or risk, they will more easily enjoy learning. When under too much stress, the brain sputters. Some researchers call this "downshifting." [17] When this happens, usually there are feelings of helplessness and fatigue. Few can enjoy problem solving or learning in such a state.

On the other hand, promoting a state of "relaxed alertness" is optimal. This is a feeling of being calm while maintaining an alert, focused attention. It has been defined as "the state in which we experience low threat and high challenge at the same time. A runner at high speed is both relaxed and performing at her maximum. Threat and fatigue inhibit brain functioning whereas challenge accompanied by safety and belief in one's abilities leads to peak performance." [18]

By helping our children develop relaxed alertness, they will not only be more likely to enjoy mental challenges, but they will acquire more psychic space available for creative expression as well. Here are four things you can do to promote relaxed alertness:

- See the whole child, with all her strengths and talents, especially when she is trying your patience or doing something contrary to what you expect.
- As much as you can, provide for some decompression time before he has to do homework, give a performance, or take a test. Emphasize physical activity to dissipate stress whenever possible.

- Help your child complete tasks on time. Procrastination only adds stress.
- Key into any learning or artistic goals your child has expressed. Surprise him with a set of paintbrushes, for instance. Encourage playful experimentation in what your child has expressed curiosity about.

Home Creativity Centers

In addition to psychic space, kids need physical spaces that support creative expression. While screen machines are fairly accessible, especially televisions, a lot of time clothes for dress-up, paints, markers, clay, or other foundation materials for creativity are not. You can set up a few "creativity centers" around your home to make it easier for your child to engage his or her creativity. You don't have to do anything fancy. In the kitchen or the garage or the laundry room—preferably somewhere with a linoleum floor—you can put up an Arts and Craft Table. Here would go all sorts of fun materials for painting, coloring, sculpting, making collages, or seasonal art projects. Your child could create cards to send out to relatives or paste family photos in an album. In the family room or the child's bedroom, you could have a special desk or area called The Writer's Nook. Here your child could make up stories and poems, pretend to be an important journalist, or with older children or teens, actually write a letter to an editor or an essay to submit for publication.

It could be a fun family project to redesign your home to include more opportunities for creative expression. Given the space, your child's creativity will blossom. You probably will be pleasantly surprised as you witness your child's self-identity blooming as well.

Parenting as an Art Form

Parenting is a continual creative process. We are constantly inventing better ways for our kids. We use "out of the box thinking" everyday as we separate squabbling siblings, get dinner on the table in the midst of helping with homework, or figure out a smoother morning routine. Matthew Fox considers parenting "a special art." He writes, "A parent must do strong things at times, pay mindful attention, be alert, loving and defensive of one's children, protecting them from the onslaughts from advertisers and media, communications that would distort a child's view of creation. And yet, a parent must also let her or his child go to experience life on their own. There is a special art, therefore, to being a parent, an art that is not different from any other act of compassion: an art that combines heart and head, love and intelligence, communication and silence." [19]

If we approach parenting as an art form we can counteract the industry-generated culture that often "distorts a child's view of creation." As we value our parental creative expression, our unique way of combining head and heart, we help our kids retain a healthy view of creation. God's creation depends on our creativity. As we use it, our kids see that they can use theirs as well. Appreciating our inherent parental creativity, even in the small things we do each day, also gives us more energy to act on behalf of our children. As we discussed in Chapter Two: Our children are not blank sheets of paper on which we write. Rather, they are Nature's works of art. It's not about us making them into anything. Rather, it's about us making ourselves into the best parents we can be. Creative expression helps with this. Like a choreographer who orchestrates a move and then adjusts it because something was not quite right, we can observe if an insight we had was accurate or if a spontaneous idea we acted on was worth repeating. If not, tapping into our creativity, we adjust. Consider what your creative self would do each time you think, "I don't know how I'm going to do such and such." As a single mother of two young sons I thought that I would go nuts if I didn't have a television. When their father wanted the TV in our divorce settlement, I was sure I couldn't get through a harried evening without one. But I got a big surprise.

Almost immediately, without access to TV, my boys, then two and four, started playing together more cooperatively. Their fussing and fighting disappeared almost overnight. After just one week without TV, I noticed a marked increase in their creativity and ability to come up with their own ideas. After two weeks, *I* realized that I didn't need a TV in order for me to keep them busy and out of my hair. Even when I got home from work, tired and cranky, I was able to come up with an idea that engaged the boys. It was as if my creative self had to kick into gear. She had no choice.

Each evening the boys usually helped me prepare a meal. I didn't need them out of my way so much because they were more cooperative. After being in child care all day, they liked doing things with me. And to my delight, I so enjoyed these precious times with them. Often we had dinner by candle light—even though hot dogs or macaroni and cheese. Then we would do something together. We played classical music on the FM radio station and pretended to be at concerts, talking about what instrument was our favorite. We went out in the warm spring rain and collected rain water for our houseplants and watered them. We used my camera to take photos and created photo essays. We did all sorts of easy things like this. It was no problem thinking of something to do after I figured out that by engaging my creativity, I enhanced theirs, and made my life so much easier in the process.

The greatest and most powerful lesson I learned from this experience was that I came to trust my creative expression. The more I relied on it, the better it served me. I saw first-hand how it catalyzed ideas. It brought me and my sons closer. It empowered us in our different ways and made the hours of 5-8 p.m. more fun than I would have believed possible. At the end of a long day, they went to sleep knowing they were loved and that they were creative and smart little boys.

Back then, I was a long way from thinking of my parenting as an art form. I was just thinking about what I could do without a television until I could afford to buy one. Creative expression, though, had a different agenda. Once started, it didn't want to quit. After a busy work day, I actually found myself enjoying thinking about the fun things I wanted to do with my sons when we got home. In fact, I didn't get a television until the boys were older and in school. By then, I knew that creative expression, theirs and mine, could get us through anything. The industry-generated culture, for us, became the emperor with no clothes—silly and stupid most of the time—certainly not nearly as fun or as interesting as our own creativity.

As you contemplate the information and ideas in this chapter, turn your attention to your creative spirit. Feed this vital human need. Consider your parenting as a sacred art form. You won't be disappointed. Neither will your children.

To Catalyze Your Creative Expression

- Nurture your ideals. What is it that you *really* want to do? That gives you joy? How can you take a step in that direction?

- Ask a good friend to write you a letter, emphasizing your creative talents and skills. Read it often until you don't discount anything that is said in the letter—when your inner talk absolutely agrees with it.

- Do something new, just for you. Is your creative self itching to begin something—maybe a new garden area, a fresh look with some new scarves, or an ordered garage? Listen to an inner urge to try something you've been putting off, like a special course or a health club membership.

- Dabble. Play around with watercolors one week, writing poetry the next. No one has to see the products of your dabbling. Pay attention to what you say to yourself about your creative expressions.

- Bring in beauty. Clearing off a cluttered countertop or perking up a room with a bouquet of flowers can inspire creative ideas. What simple thing can you do each day that will add beauty to your environment?

- Practice speaking your truth. It will set you free, as well as free up your creative expression.

- Honor your creative expression by taking your talents seriously.

7

The Fifth Essential Need:
Contribution as Relationship

We cannot serve at a distance. We can only serve that to which we are profoundly connected, that which we are willing to touch.

Joan Borysenko[1]

Consider the common thread in these examples:

Eight four-year-old girls gather together at a birthday party to watch a video of *The Little Mermaid*.

A couple, newly-married, decide to pick up a pizza and a video on a Friday evening to unwind after a busy week.

Two sixteen-year-old boys wake up at 3 a. m. to get in line for the opening of a popular movie.

A college professor shows his students the movie *Platoon*, to spur a discussion about the Vietnam War.

In each of these examples, there is a mutual sharing of industry-generated messages. In this sharing, meaning is created. As we gather in homes or in classrooms to enjoy a movie for its entertainment value or scrutinize it for its historical implications, we make meaning together. That meaning may or may not be *personally* meaningful. For instance, there is a big difference when kids watch a movie with no adult to filter the information and when they are with a parent who makes comments while watching or in a classroom with a teacher guiding the process. With conversation, the meaning derived from industry-generated messages will likely be scrutinized and absorbed in light of personal significance. How kids choose to interpret the industry-generated messages will become more conscious to them as well. When children are mere spectators, though, the meaning being made is more unconscious or unobvious since there is little or no human relating going on. When this happens, over and over again, through years of movies, television programs, and video games, kids can lose touch with their role as contributors. Since, in passive viewing, they aren't contributing ideas to a conversation about the screen images, they become increasingly distanced from their real human need to participate in life and contribute to it. And even when the kids talk about screen content among themselves—i.e., without the guidance of caring adults—often they can't easily ascribe personal significance to what they are seeing. Without understanding the personal value of the industry-generated culture through the lens of adult guidance, children and teens are distanced from their role of contributors to society. Their conversations revolve around industry-generated topics, led by marketing agendas. How meaningful is the meaning they collaboratively create in this way?

Kids also learn what is important by choices adults make for them. In one of the examples above, four-year-old girls come together as a group to watch a video at a birthday party. This is a common practice today. Typically, the adults are in another room while the children watch. Even if it's a "harmless video," the children don't have an opportunity to talk about what they are seeing and ascribe significance to it according to socially acceptable role models. Because the adults have chosen to show it at a special event, the youngsters can unconsciously make the assumption that the video is of very much importance. Watching *The Little Mermaid* for two hours together as a group, the little girls share an implicit understanding that this is what groups of children do to have fun together. Yet, if the girls don't spend an equal amount, or more time, actually relating to each other in playing a game or joining forces for, say, a treasure hunt, they have little real opportunities to create meaning together apart from the industry-generated priorities.

Rather than participating meaningfully in activities that would help them grow into participating adults in the real world, the little girls learn that participating in life means consuming images. As our children and teens watch movies together, shop malls as primary ways of socializing, talk about TV programs on the playground, or spend time after school playing video games together, they mutually share the content created for them by a business. It then becomes their business to keep that content alive in their interactions with each other in order to be accepted. After all, a part of all relationships is the sharing of common concerns. When industry-generated concerns overshadow anything else, they become a large part of the content in friendships and peer interactions. Contribution to something outside of themselves or their relationship takes a back seat.

In order for kids to see and experience themselves as

contributors, they must be able to see and experience themselves as people capable of relating. The tidal wave displacement of normal human relatedness in an industry-generated culture has devastating effects. For instance, four hours daily in front of screen machines limits kids' opportunities to negotiate or cooperate; to work jointly to solve problems; or to listen carefully and summarize another's point of view. These skills require human interactions.

Children must also experience human interactions to know how to handle negative ones. The television doesn't kick a three year-old and say, "I want my toy back," as a peer would. A video game won't make fun of a fourteen year-old, but a peer might. Particularly disturbing is the impact during the early years when the development of the ability to control behavior depends upon appropriate social interactions. As discussed in Chapter Three, most experts agree that achieving emotion regulation is dependent upon early social interactions. As the child's brain matures, complex layers of emotion control become possible.[2]

Without such social learning experiences emotional health is stunted. Disruption of normal socialization processes in an industry-generated culture has severe consequences. Children don't spend enough time relating to each other. And when they do, often it's about industry-generated topics. It may seem obvious, but how can children and teens view themselves as participants in life and contributors to the common good when they aren't participating in life or contributing to the common good?

We all know that a human need is to have healthy relationships. We understand that another important human need is to contribute to something larger than ourselves. Together they form the fifth essential need, contribution as relationship. In a healthy relationship, either to self, others, or to the world, there exists an important component of healthy contribution. Since we feel connected, we think a lot about what we can give. In friendships and intimate relationships, we want to contribute to the life of the other person, as well as to the life of the relationship. We find meaning and value in giving. This is a mark of maturity and a major goal of personal development. We also find inspiration in our loving relationships. They ignite our wish to contribute to something purposeful that exists outside of the relationship. In fact, human relationships need to be connected to something larger than each of the individuals in that relationship. A couple shares joint goals in rearing children or service goals, perhaps, if they decide not to have children. A group of friends come together to make weekly dinners for a friend who has become too ill to do it for herself. Whenever people share loving bonds, they form unifying bonds with each other for the purpose of contribution.

It's human to want to make a difference. But in an industry-generated culture, we parents have to clear the path for our kids to know this. We have to become more intentional about helping our children experience their connection to the larger world. As screen machines dominate children's lives, how can they ever feel their connection to that world?

Without connection to and time exploring and engaging the natural world, how do children desire to take care of the environment? How do they decide to contribute to the living system of which they are a part? In front of screen machines, they can't recognize themselves as human. They need to relate to people for that affirmation. We may think, "My child will play a Gameboy only a little while I shop at the mall." Or we may agree with the mother of three children who bought a car VCR to use on long trips, "It turns the drive into a dream date for my husband and me. We actually get to talk up front while the kids are busy watching in back." [3] But time disconnected from people means children are plugged into an industry-generated culture. If we can't expect our kids to participate in conversations with us in daily activities, how can we expect them to value the worth of contributing their talents and skills to society? Allowing them to consume screen images at the expense of relating to real people is a dangerous proposition for them and for our culture.

In this chapter we explore how parents can help their children understand themselves as contributors and feel the real need to contribute outside of themselves. The first section examines the concept of "personal adequacy" and its implications as the foundation for this fifth essential human need. Then, we look at how learning to contribute also strengthens important internal qualities of resiliency, relational thinking, and motivation to share. Finally, we explore the concept of "parent as servant leader," and how it can assist us in modeling contribution for our children, as well as what we inherently gain by being a "servant leader" in our families.

Personal Adequacy: The Foundation

The first four of the Vital Five human needs: a loving parent-child bond, an inner life, image-making, and creative expression enable us to form healthy relationships and contribute meaningfully to something greater than ourselves. These needs must be actively supported to develop the understanding of contribution as relationship. Without them, children can become self-indulgent and self-centered. With them, children become capable of developing self-efficacy, a prerequisite to forming healthy relationships and contributing meaningfully to society. Studies have shown that persons with high self-efficacy have the following traits. [4]

They can:

- Set high goals, knowing they will succeed.
- Visualize success. (People with low self-efficacy visualize failure.)
- Possess skills to manage emotions and can use such skills under taxing conditions.
- Discover quickly what strategies work for them in a broad range of situations.
- Work hard toward a goal.
- Possess a positive attitude.

These characteristics not only help a person to succeed in life. They also set the foundation for critical communication skills and feelings of self-worth that are needed to be in successful, intimate relationships; long-term friendships; and amicable work associations. With self-efficacy comes a solid sense of self-worth. Psychologist Albert Bandura calls self-efficacy a "self-referent phenomenon." [5] That means a person with it "is largely independent of pressure from someone or something outside of the individual…It is their own beliefs, thoughts, and moral or ethical fiber that gives meaning and value to external events." [6]

Another way to put this is that the person feels adequate within him or herself. Such people can then ascribe meaning or significance to what they do and why they do it. They are internally directed. Their sense of self is not determined by what others think, say, or do. Conversely, because they can be detached from others' opinions, people who have a sense of adequacy feel united with others. Since they don't need to prove themselves, they can listen better to what others are really saying. They don't have to do any one-upping because their ego is in check. With self-efficacy, children and teens would be doing a lot less bullying, for instance, because they wouldn't need to dominate others to derive a sense of personal agency. Their personal power would stem from an authentic sense of self. Cooperation between or among individuals is much more the norm when they all feel personally adequate. The research on this subject demonstrates that "adequate persons have much concern for other people, which shows itself in humanitarian interests...They are often motivated by love, understanding, and compassion...They do not find it necessary to use others for solely personal gratification and, as a consequence, can devote themselves more to other people. They have the capacity to give of themselves."[7]

Giving of ourselves without a sense of personal adequacy is giving from a victim mentality. The giving is not given freely. On the other hand, a sense of personal adequacy frees a person to make appropriate choices for developing and maintaining healthy relationships. It provides the impetus to move outside of self and enjoy the process of contribution—whether to another individual, a group, or to society.

Serving Life

The little child's chubby legs were the only thing I could see through the wire mesh of the large wastebasket. From my angle of viewing, his head and torso were invisible. Then I saw his curly, dark hair as he bent down and worked hard to pick up a candy bar wrapper someone had thrown, missing the receptacle. Once he grabbed on to it, he stretched, got up on his tip toes as far as he could and very gently, with utmost care, released it into the basket. Running over to his parents a few feet away, he proudly announced, "See, I keep America clean." His parents responded with smiles, a hug, and positive comments.

This little one's sense of personal adequacy was definitely intact. He noticed the litter. He wanted to do something about it. And he did do something about it. Modeling parental behavior and training, he felt delight and a healthy pride in making a contribution. Even at age three, he was learning to make a difference to something beyond himself.

The impetus to contribute comes from a felt connection. In her inspiring book, *My Grandfather's Blessings*, Rachel Naomi Remen points out that "service does not need to be taught. It may be a natural impulse in all people."[8] As parents our primary work then, is not so much to coerce service out of our kids, as it is to cultivate it within them. Remen tells a story from the notable Austrian psychiatrist, Dr. Rudolf Dreikurs:

> "In *Children, the Challenge*, his revolutionary book on parenting, Dreikurs tells a story about a mother returning from the store and putting her bags of groceries down on the kitchen table. She opens the refrigerator, takes out the empty plastic containers that hold the eggs, and sets them on the table next to the bags. Then she begins to put groceries away. Returning from the pantry, she sees that her two-year-old has climbed onto the table, opened the egg carton and, two handed, is transferring one egg at

a time into the egg container. 'No, no,' she cries in alarm, 'that's not for little girls, you'll break them,' and she lifts her daughter who has begun to cry down from the table and puts away the rest of the eggs herself. Fourteen years later she will probably still be putting the eggs away herself and perhaps cleaning up her daughter's room as well.'"9

Standing by while our kids awkwardly attempt tasks can take a lot of patience. Holding back our comments while they learn how to do something can take a lot of self-discipline. But if we manage to delegate and let our kids do a few things, they will get in touch with their inherent need to contribute. Besides, we actually strengthen our relationship with them when we allow them to be of service. Here in this fifth essential need, we have come full circle from the first one—a loving parent-child bond. By contributing in small ways through household chores and specific tasks like taking the dog for a daily walk or emptying the dishwasher, we give opportunities for strengthening the parent-child relationship. The more they contribute to the family, the stronger our bond with them will be. And the stronger their sense of belonging will be.

The first community the child must see him or herself a part of is the home community. You probably haven't thought much about your home being a community. But it is. It is the first opportunity for children to learn the value of contribution and where they can experience all the good feelings that come with contributing to something beyond themselves. In his book *Surplus Powerlessness*, Michael Lerner writes that historically "individual families were not seen as the purpose of life, nor did anyone suppose that an individual relationship made sense by itself. Rather families were consecrated and given meaning precisely to the extent that they were seen as vital parts of a larger and non-family-based vision. A family got its purpose by virtue of its relationship to this larger community of meaning. The family would raise children who could then enter into this larger community, and the community would support that venture because the children were seen as part of the ongoing life of the community. Life's hardships and defeats and disappointments in each family were shared by the community as its own problems and not just 'personal problems.'" [10]

In an industry-generated culture, however, it's different. While most schools still see families as "vital parts of a larger...vision," many families don't see themselves as such. Parent involvement in schools has increasingly declined as our society puts more stress on families. With time being a precious commodity, many parents can't participate in the life of the larger community, even though they might like to. Instead of community activities adding to family aliveness, in many instances, it diminishes it. In too many cases, the family's problems remain personal ones. Social agencies may also view parents as a vital part of the community, but they frequently can't convey that vision to stressed-out parents. Many parents, then, approach social agencies with the expectation that the agencies will solve their problems. They don't see themselves as collaborators with the agencies in finding solutions. It's the same with schools. A lot of parents approach the school environment thinking about what they can receive for their children and not from the perspective of what they can give to the school to make it a better place for their children. It's not the family's fault that their connections to these institutions are tenuous.

Because most schools and social agencies are set up from a mechanistic model, rather than a living system one, they can't easily act as a heartfelt, supportive community—what most parents really need.

There are complex reasons why parents are more stressed and why social services and institutions like schools can't easily authentically support parents—from rising costs of living, to more single parents trying to make it alone, to the collapsing infrastructures of many public schools. But one important reason must be recognized. The industry-generated culture makes it easy to stay inside our homes or our rooms isolated from others. Many get a pseudo-sense of community becoming involved in the lives of soap opera characters or celebrity divorces. Computer activities like gaming or shopping fill up a lot of leisure time. If it's easier to stay home in front of a screen machine rather than engage in community events, children can't easily understand the need to contribute to something larger than the family. The family is it.

If you are a busy parent and have a difficult time getting out of the house for school events or other activities important in your child's life, don't be hard on yourself. Start where you're at and go from there. In viewing the family as a community, there are things you can do in your home that would instill in children a sense of being a part of that "larger vision." For instance, one or two nights away from any screen machine and doing projects together as a family will give kids of any age a great feeling of contributing to something bigger than themselves. It doesn't have to be a fancy project to be effective. To us it might be a chore to clean out a closet, but to a seven year-old it's a way to order his or her toys and pull a few to give to needy children. A sixteen year-old may fuss about having to paste old photos in a family album. But given the expectation to do so, she may become engrossed and excited about the family history she is learning. We have to bring opportunities for contribution to our kids. We are guardians of their ability to serve the world. No matter how small and insignificant these types of family activities may seem, they ought not to be dismissed. From your child's perspective, they are crucially important because they teach about authentic participation.

Your family is not only a community, it's a living system. Like any living organism, each part must support the whole. If this isn't happening the whole isn't as alive or as effective as it can be. Each cell in our bodies, when healthy, contributes to our overall health. A cell that's become self-absorbed and doesn't know how to cooperate effectively with the cells around it is a cancer cell. It's lost its purpose. Rather than adding to the body's vitality, it decreases it. Children who don't learn how to contribute to their families decrease the potential and aliveness of the entire family.

As children participate in the life of the family by giving to it, they begin to understand themselves as part of the human family. They connect to parents and siblings in deeper ways and feel connected to their family more deeply. One couple I coached provided a "contribution opportunity," as they put it, and were moved by how it affected their children. At the time of initiating it, their sons were twelve and fourteen. Because these parents both had busy work schedules they decided to let their kids know how they could support them. On a weekly basis the family got together for a conversation that went something like this:

Dad: "I want you to know that I would really appreciate your help cleaning out the garage next Saturday. Will that work with your soccer practice, Neal? You both can help me organize that new shelving. I can show you how it works. It's really cool."

Mom: "This week, Tuesday and Thursday, will be extra busy work days for me. My boss wants me to facilitate some important meetings, so I'll be getting home late. Tim, I will want you to put the casserole I made in the oven on Tuesday so it can be cooking while I'm on my way home from work and you can start the salad. Neal, you can do the same on Thursday. Now is there any special things going on for you this week that you need extra support with?"

Tim: "I have a geography test on Friday. I was hoping Dad could help me study for it Thursday night."

Dad: "No problem. Since Mom will be a little late that night, I'll try to be home a little earlier."

Neal: "I have a big game in two weeks and coach says we have to practice on our own this week besides regular practice. Can someone drive me to the soccer field on Monday and Wednesday?"

In this type of supportive atmosphere, the boys found that as they gave support, they also received it. With more understanding of give and take, the boys started thinking beyond themselves more often. As they navigated adolescence together, this family worked together on alleviating stresses and helping each other through difficult times. The boys trusted their parents to be there for them. The parents spurred on their sons' maturity by expecting them to contribute to the family and appreciating them for doing so.

As our kids learn authentic participation within the family, they acquire the motivation to contribute to life beyond the family. Pushing children or teens into "voluntary" service won't work well if they have not first experienced contribution opportunities within the family. Many high schools today have a community service component as a graduation requirement. This is a wonderful thing. But how authentic will their contribution be if the teens don't experience themselves as connected to that which they are serving? For service outside of the home to be personally meaningful, kids must learn about contribution as relationship. That's best done by contributing to those they love and relate to each day. For our children to serve life authentically they must start with the home community, the place where their life began.

Contributing Keeps Us Connected

Recent studies show that children's brains are "hardwired to connect." That is, children are biologically predisposed for close attachments to other people and for attaching to meaning beyond themselves.[11] We discussed the critical need for bonding with loving parents in Chapter Three. Children also need a social environment that supports their close attachments as well as loving adults that guide them to seek answers about life's deepest questions. For this reason more researchers and educators emphasize that social connectedness plays a big role in appropriate emotional health and the development of living from a sense of higher purpose.

The Commission on Children at Risk sponsored by YMCA of USA, Dartmouth Medical School, and the Institute for American Values brought neuroscientists, leading medical doctors, and social scientists together in an unprecedented collaboration in 2003. The commission strongly recommended that our society pay more attention to young people's moral and spiritual needs because so many of our youth are disconnected—from themselves and from society.[12]

Despite a decade of economic growth that resulted in fewer children living in poverty, large and growing numbers of American children and adolescents are suffering from mental health problems. Scholars at the National Research Council estimate that at least one of every four adolescents in the U.S. is currently at risk of not achieving productive adulthood. Twenty-one percent of U.S. children ages nine to seventeen have a diagnosable mental disorder or addiction; eight percent of high school students suffer from clinical depression, and about twenty percent of students report seriously having considered suicide in the past year. The average U.S. child in the 1980s reported more anxiety than the average child psychiatric patient in the 1950s.[13]

Social Connectedness

These sad statistics demonstrate the critical need kids have today for authentic social connectedness. One step parents can take is to talk more about the nature of altruism—what it is and why it's important in the life of every human. Dr. Stephanie Brown, a psychologist at the University of Michigan in Ann Arbor, has found that altruism, defined as providing social support, is apparently good not just for the recipients but for the individual altruist, too. Her five-year study showed that older people who reported helping someone else just once a year were likely to live longer, as were husbands and wives who were able to make their spouse feel loved and cared for. Dr. Brown suggests that "giving may induce positive feelings, relieving stress and buffering cardiovascular effects."[14] In fact, connecting and contributing to others can help us live longer. There is a body of research that suggests isolated individuals vastly increase their odds of an early death by showing signs of a lowered immune system and self-defeating behaviors.[15]

Talking about the concept of unconditional love can also validate the importance of social connectedness and inspire kids to contribute. For instance, teens and parents alike may find it fascinating that there exists an Institute for Research on Unlimited Love. That the medical profession takes love of others seriously can be an interesting topic for family conversation. The institute's visionary founder and president is Dr. Stephen Post, who teaches bioethics in the School of Medicine at Case Western University in Cleveland where the not-for-profit is based. He says it has two main goals: to support research and education on the nature and expression of unlimited love, or the "total constant love for every person with no exception," and "to better understand our capacities for participation in unlimited love as the ultimate purpose of our lives." "Until now," he admits, "compassionate love and altruism have been the territory of theologians and philosophers. But in a world where most science is applied to human deficits or disease, it makes sense to also look at the positive aspects of human nature scientifically."[16]

Parents can share this type of information with their teens and discuss what they think about it. You can talk about times when your kids did something for another that caused them to have positive feelings. Older kids and teens have probably heard the phrase, "Perform random acts of kindness." By asking them to do some every week and talking with us about how they felt afterwards, we reinforce the personal satisfaction gleaned from helping out. With this feeling comes a sense of being connected to others, allowing our children to experience themselves in new ways. Feelings of relatedness play a big role in helping children and teens become self-directed, competent individuals, capable of making wise choices for themselves and others. In fact, relatedness is considered a basic psychological need because the experience of belonging provides the emotional security required to actively venture out in the world and be productive in it.[17]

Connecting to Three Inner Strengths

When humans contribute to others or to a cause outside of themselves, they build several internal strengths. Resiliency is one of them. Resiliency is the ability to stay with a challenge, no matter what, and to bounce back from adversity, stronger from the experience. It's a critical quality in order to be an effective problem-solver or successful in any career. Since life frequently throws us curve balls, resiliency aids our flexibility to keep moving toward our goals, despite setbacks. Bonnie Benard in her book, *Resiliency: What We Have Learned*, cites hundreds of studies that have found that "for just about any population of children that research has found to be at greater risk than normal for later problems—children who experience divorce, have attention deficit disorder, suffer developmental delays, become delinquent, run away, were placed in foster care, were born to teen mothers, were members of gangs, were sexually abused, had substance-abusing or mentally ill families, and grew up in poverty…what appears to be crucial for these young people are caring relationships, high expectations, and opportunities to participate and contribute, whether in their families, schools, or communities." [18] Research shows problem behaviors decline and resiliency grows the more kids participate and contribute. This is vitally important and hopeful research. And it makes a lot of sense. We see our children blossom in their feelings of self-worth and dignity when they help around the house. We notice the pride when our teen volunteers to be a Big Brother or Big Sister. The feelings of deep satisfaction of making a positive difference are accompanied by a learned inner strength. By giving to others, kids build their capacity to give to themselves in times of stress. Contribution acts like a set of weights to exercise human resiliency muscles.

Another internal strength built through authentic contribution is what is known as "relational reality." This is the ability to see beyond ones' own individual needs to another's. It's not always easy to do in a society that puts a lot of emphasis on the individual. In his book *The Saturated Self*, Kenneth Gergen considers how we think about our individual needs and the needs of others:

> "One ponders, 'How should I live my life?' and considers the 'desire for fulfilling work,' 'needs for loving relationships,' 'hopes for children,' or 'wants for financial security.' One pauses to consider how the day or the evening should be spent, and again account is taken of one's wishes, needs, hopes, and fears. Such contemplations are commonplace. Yet consider some contrasting possibilities. How often do we ask, for example, 'I wonder what my family will do

with its life?' 'What will my community do this month?' or 'How will my marriage fare today?' We find it 'only natural' to contemplate our own personal desires, needs, wants, and fears and to direct our lives accordingly. It is awkward and confusing to lay self aside and to focus on the broader units of being. Relationships come and go, we believe. . .the individual self is the center of society." [19]

We live in what has been called a post-modern world in which the individual takes precedence over the whole. It shouldn't be surprising then that even our inner speech often is biased in favor of our own needs over others' needs, even as adults. But when we contribute to others we are tuned into their needs and practice thinking in terms of a more interdependent reality, as opposed to an independent one. For instance, in our daily conversations, we either connect authentically with others or we don't. Eye contact, body language, voice patterns, and listening techniques can determine if we are contributing a sense of our self to the conversation. Do we see our interactions with others as interdependent, equally focused on the other as much as we are focused on what we want to get out of the conversation or receive from the other person?

Children and teens can learn to develop relational skills by being more aware of what they are actually contributing in terms of active listening, questioning, and awareness when interacting with others. One practice we can have our children do is to observe people talking to one another and noticing how their voice rhythms and body gestures either aid the connection or disrupt it. Anthropologist Eliott Chapple found that adolescents who were considered popular had a greater ability to adapt their interaction pattern to match others. Adolescents who had little ability to adjust their pattern of speech and voice were not only more socially isolated, they showed more displays of violence. They literally couldn't connect with others.[20]

If you observe the energy between two people, you can determine if the contributing by one person is being accepted graciously by the other. For instance, if one person forces an idea or contributes to the conversation in a way that diminishes the other person, the energy between the two people will decrease, also. When two people are "on the same wavelength" and there is a mutual sharing with mutual respect, the energy remains high and the conversation can energize both parties. Older children and teens can notice this in their own interactions and observe it in interactions between family members and friends. Older children and teens can learn to know when they are positively contributing to others and when they aren't. They can assess whether what was offered by another person seemed right for them. As they become more relationally aware, kids also build an understanding of what authentic contribution means to them.

A third internal quality that is built though contribution is the motivation to share. In an industry-generated culture that equates possession with power, this is a particularly challenging concept for many children. Young children, of course, are less likely to willingly share and need instruction to do so. As children grow, the internal drive to share grows as they develop friendships and important bonds with others. Social context plays an important role in the willingness to share. For instance, when a teacher sets up a safe classroom atmosphere free of ridicule, children are more likely to risk sharing a new idea. Sharing with others can make us feel vulnerable. It often brings out our fears and insecurities. Because we want what we are offering to be accepted, it can be personally offensive if it isn't.

Yet, sharing with others can also help make us feel valuable. To overcome students' lack of motivation for learning, some schools have found success in having the children share their work with others. Many teachers I know will have their students read to other teachers, the janitor, or even the food service staff. Many youngsters get excited about sharing their new skills with others who show them encouragement. One high school teacher found that "when students know that their project or performance will be presented to an audience outside the classroom, they are inspired to produce work of the highest quality."[21]

When parents make it a regular expectation that children contribute to the family and do consistent acts of social service, we help them see that sharing of ourselves doesn't have to be scary. It can truly feel rewarding. A child who contributes as a normal part of his or her self-expression develops an internal guidance system for giving to others. The drive to share springs forth from a felt need. It doesn't have to be imposed. The child naturally develops purpose for sharing. Purpose is a powerful director, moving us from our present awareness to a new behavior or attitude. With purpose to share, a child shares more often, thus maintaining motivation to share over time.

Effective ways we can support children's motivation to share:

Keep the mood light and the atmosphere non-restrictive.

Just like the wise teacher who creates a classroom atmosphere that minimizes risk, so too, in our homes we can support our children's desire to share by making it comfortable for them to do so. This doesn't mean being overly permissive. Rather, within a set of boundaries, parents can support a relaxed home atmosphere, conducive to sharing. That means reducing the pressure to share. Putting on the pressure usually backfires in the long-run. As psychologist Edward L. Deci, at the University of Rochester advises, "Sure, there's such a thing as being graceful under pressure. But the point is that the more pressure you put on people, the less likely it is that they they'll be graceful, or interested, or feel good about themselves." [22] While we don't want to coddle a child, we don't want to flatten his or her self-worth, either. By creating a supportive atmosphere and inviting children and teens to give us their opinions or to share what they are feeling about their latest accomplishments, we give them a chance to take a risk of revealing more of themselves. When they find that there are no penalties for doing so, they, of course, share more willingly.

Consider more "Vital Appreciation."

Writing in his classic book in 1906, *Democracy and Education*, John Dewey emphasizes the need for loving adults to express appreciation to children. "A youth who has had repeated experience of the full meaning of the value of kindliness toward others built into his disposition has a measure of the worth of generous treatment of others. Without this vital appreciation, the duty and virtue of unselfishness, impressed upon him by others as a standard remains purely a matter of symbols which he cannot adequately translate into realities." [23] When parents demonstrate appreciation to their children, it makes giving to others real for them. It catalyzes their ability to become more generous.

Discuss the dynamic aspect of life.

If your child is reluctant to share, affirm how natural that is as we all have days when we would rather be alone or we would rather not reach out to another person, for whatever reason. Life changes constantly. So do we. Our motivation to share changes and there will come a better time to share. By stressing this to our youngsters and giving them permission to share when they feel right about it, we will eventually increase their internal drive to share. It's another way to take the external pressure off and nudge our kids into taking up the responsibility to share for themselves.

Model our own motivation to share.

If we have the courage to let others see our excitement, we show that excitement is of value. When you are excited about sharing something with your kids, let your enthusiasm show. Do you have a new assignment at church that will allow you to contribute something interesting to your Sunday school class? Explain what motivates you about this new assignment to your children. Are you enthused about a new project at work? Discuss with your family what motivates you to share more of yourself with others. Let your children hear what propels you to contribute to others and society. They'll be motivated by it!

Staying Vigilant in an Industry-Generated Culture

These three internal qualities: resiliency, relational reality, and motivation to share can be severely impacted in an industry-generated culture. It can seem like everywhere kids look, they get misdirecting messages, countering the importance of contribution and the meaning of relationships.

1. Instead of affirming to children their need to develop their resiliency, the industry-generated culture brings countless messages that implicitly say, "Stay within the comfort zone we define for you. Keep doing the same things over and over. We will tell you what is cool and worthwhile to do. You don't have to think about this for yourself. You don't need to focus on your own internal strength."

2. Instead of nurturing skills for understanding their relational reality, the industry-generated culture implicitly repeats: "Don't think of others, think only of yourself. That's the way to be cool. Focus on yourself, especially the superficial aspects of yourself. Is your hair properly done? Do you wear the right clothes? If you answer yes to these types of questions, then 'good' relationships will just happen for you. And if they don't, then keep looking for the right thing to buy to make it happen. It's not necessary to focus attention on your inner capacity for relating to others, or to develop that capacity."

3. Instead of providing impetus to share of one's self with others, the industry-generated culture advises: "Be like anybody else but yourself. Your unique abilities and your unique presence to those in your family and community are not important. It's how you are like the image we give you that's important. If you need to

give something to someone, here are the things you can buy, already made. And they're good and desirable because everybody else is buying and giving the same thing."

If it seems like a daunting parental task to counter such messages on a daily basis, that's because it is. As we have seen in various examples in other chapters, parental influence has limitations. Cultural influences also shape minds, impact emotional capacities, and spiritual depth. The culture in which children live must be saying roughly the same thing as the parents most of the time or the children experience a dissonance between the two messages that they are not prepared to handle. And the industry-generated culture clearly isn't, by and large, saying the same things as parents.

Research consistently reveals that "social contexts that engender conflicts between basic needs set up the conditions for alienation and psychopathology."[24] The social context of the industry-generated culture sets up continual dissonance for our kids. They have a human need to belong, after all. They want to belong to their peer group. But unfortunately, it's more than likely that their peer group belongs to the industry-generated culture. Their peers may think it's cool not to share, to be unkind, or even to bully continually. We parents are trying to teach kids healthy ways to be in relationships and to contribute. But much of the cultural air kids breathe negates our messages. If we don't do something, our kids grow confused and possibly alienated with psychological problems.

Since we can't readily change the industry-generated culture, we must first accept the fact that there will be dissonance. The values and attitudes we are teaching our kids are likely not to be upheld by the industry-generated culture. In accepting this, we can become more deliberate about talking with our kids about their confusion. How unfair it is that some of their friends do such and such and that they can't, for example. It's critical that we keep a lot of conversations going around this issue, find out what our kids are thinking, and how they are feeling about themselves in the midst of their confusion and feelings of being singled out as different from their peers.

Alan Atkinson, a PCI trained parent coach on Maui and a father of five children, explains it this way: "When dissonance happens, the opportunity to learn also happens at the same time. A parent can help or hinder this process by his/her reactions to the child as the child attempts to rearrange their worldview. If the parent expects the child to learn without being confused or without the need to figure things out, the child could begin to think of him or herself 'stupid' for not getting it. If the parent encourages the child throughout the process of sorting out the confusion, it seems the child would begin to gain confidence in their ability to learn and work through other dissonance opportunities on his or her own." [25]

If we stay vigilant and consistent in helping our kids sort through confusing messages as they grow up in an industry-generated culture, they will tap into the well of knowledge and wisdom within *themselves*. They will discover that it is a normal human need to relate healthily to people. They will experience joy in their authentic contribution to others and be able to look beyond themselves to contribute to society as well.

Parent as Servant Leader

In 1977, the late Robert Greenleaf published a book that turned heads in the business world and began a quiet revolution of change within the "corporate culture." That book was *Servant Leadership: A Journey into the Nature of Legitimate Power and Greatness.* The message of the book was simple, yet profound: True leadership requires that we become servants first. Often we think of a servant as having less power than the people he or she serves. Greenleaf said just the opposite. He pointed out that a wise leader puts the people he or she serves first. By contributing to others, the leader demonstrates real power. Greenleaf's concept of servant leadership "begins with the natural feeling that one wants to serve, to serve *first.* The conscious choice brings one to aspire to lead. That person is sharply different from one who is *leader* first, perhaps because of the need to assuage an unusual power drive or to acquire material possessions." [26]

Greenleaf characterizes the servant-leader as making "sure other people's priority needs are being served." He states the test of whether or not one is a servant-leader is answering these questions in the affirmative: "Do those served grow as persons? Do they, *while being served,* become healthier, wiser, freer, more autonomous, more likely themselves to become servants?" [27]

It seems to me that this concept has many applications for us as parents. For one, it affirms the inherent power in all the giving we do, all the sacrifices we make for the sake of our children. By making our children's needs the highest priority, we in a sense, lose ourselves and gain more than we ever imagined, including legitimate power in relationship to our children. Understanding ourselves as servant-leaders also affirms our primary role of guiding our children and being the strongest role model in their lives. It also addresses the humbling nature of parenthood. We learn much from our children and become bigger, more open-hearted people during the parenting journey.

Another way the concept of parent as servant-leader benefits us is that by practicing it, we can contribute even when we don't feel like it. When we are worn out after a long work day, and feel too tired to play with our child, let alone make dinner and get a bath going, we can reframe our thinking. We may be tempted to escape into the "Oh, woe is me" syndrome and focus on how difficult the situation is. But thinking of self as a servant-leader can change that. We can focus, instead, on our child's needs and feel good in our role of contributing. We can know that we put into practice leadership qualities of perseverance, stamina, self-discipline, and our own resiliency when we overcome obstacles. We can be rigorous with ourselves, as well as compassionate.

You will notice that Greenleaf refers to the feeling of serving as natural. In our industry-generated culture, we have lost that understanding. By thinking of ourselves as servant-leaders, we help our children recognize the reality of the human condition: that we need to give to others in order to be fully human.

Reflecting on Your Need for Contribution...

- Notice when you are giving out of habit or when you aren't feeling connected to the other person or to your chosen cause. Is it getting to be a chore to help out a friend? Are you sending money to an out-of-state agency, but don't know how the money is being used? Would it be better to talk with your friend about your feelings and divert the funds to a local group you know? In such instances, reflect upon what you need to change in order to re-establish your connection.

- Keep a daily log for a week on how you feel about the contributions you are making. Are they about right? Too many? Too few? What would you like to adjust so that you have a more authentic relationship to the people and ideals you are serving?

- Think of a time when you did something for someone that was no big deal to you, yet the person thanked you profusely. What did you learn about your ability to contribute from this experience?

- Think of a time when you did something for someone and no gratitude was expressed by the other person. What did you learn about your ability to contribute from this experience?

- Ask your spouse and some good friends to give you positive feedback about how they perceive you as a contributor. What do they most appreciate about your contributions to the relationship? Bask in their affirmations and take them to heart.

8

Toward a Personally-Generated Culture

For centuries we were taught to worship our ancestors and to be true to our traditions, and it was good that we did so. But now. . .we need to do something we have never had to do before. . .we must worship our descendants. We must love our grandchildren more than we love ourselves.

Jim Dator[1]

Emotionally and spiritually mature humans:

- Form caring bonds with others.
- Participate in and nurture their inner life.
- Generate their own images from within their own interiority.
- Generate purpose and meaning through their own creative expression.
- Contribute to the life and well-being of their family, community, society, and culture.

When the Vital Five are present during childhood, the child is placed on a growth trajectory that leads to maturity as a human being. And when we, as adults and parents, participate in nurturing our children with the Vital Five, we continue to develop and mature.

But there is another important aspect to nurturing our children and ourselves with the Vital Five. When the Vital Five are met, our culture is transformed. In other words, humans become capable of personally generating their own culture again. Without attention to the Vital Five, the industry-generated culture defines what it means to be human. Becoming less human, our problems only escalate.

Objectified by the over-arching culture we expect to support us, we get fooled by foolishly spending more time and attention to media messages than we spend on meeting our own real needs and those of our children. We stay baffled as to why our children can't learn, why our teens are depressed, and why we as parents, despite large measures of love and concern, are less effective than we want to be. The industry-generated culture keeps us preoccupied with worry and fear. We can't unravel why we are so tired, so frustrated, so hopeless. We have no idea where to start to make positive changes, so we don't begin. We never take a chance on a creative idea or risk speaking our truth based on our inner wisdom. We stay tethered to our screen machines and teach our kids to do the same. We no longer even have the energy to wonder what happened. We can't even recognize that something has dramatically changed.

With attention to the Vital Five, however, we can blossom as human beings and our culture transforms. For when we meet the real human needs of one person, it rubs off on all those he or she meets. An emotionally healthy and mature person brings much good in the world and provides a living model for others. Also with attention to the Vital Five, the industry-generated culture has less impact on our daily lives. As we practice and model the importance of the Vital Five to our kids, we generate a second, human culture. This culture would put our human needs first and foremost. There would be time to meet the Vital Five because everything else would be secondary. Individually and collectively, parents, and all adults, would understand the immense significance of meeting the Vital Five and the disastrous results of not attending to them.

This would be a personally-generated culture because people would directly influence attitudes and behaviors rather than large corporations. The way to rev up the collective engine for moving to a supportive, more personal culture is for parents to address the challenge questions in Chapter One head-on.

The answer is the same for each question: Practice the Vital Five.

I. *Whose messages do we want to shape the emerging identity of our children— the messages from an industry-generated culture or the messages from parents?* For our messages to reach our children in an industry-generated culture, we must practice the Vital Five.

2. *How do we help our children intentionally choose what is in their best interests when the industry-generated culture and social institutions in our communities persist in urging them to make choices not in their best interests?* By practicing the Vital Five, children will grow to know their best interests and be able to make choices to support those interests.

3. How do we nurture our children's and teens' healthy autonomy within an industry culture determined to weaken our authority and one that invests heavily in encouraging our kids to oppose what we think is best?

By practicing the Vital Five.

4. How do we parents get the relevant information we need to parent well when that information is not easily available through common mass media channels?

The core strategies of nurturing healthy children are contained in the Vital Five. They are fundamental processes that allow natural growth to occur. The rest of the information is details. In an information age, it's as important to know what information *not* to pay attention to as it is what information to attend to. If parents focus on the Vital Five they will not be confused by disinformation. Frankly, we don't need a lot of research information. What we need is *relevant* research information, along with coaching, encouragement, and understanding in how best to apply the Vital Five to our unique situations.

5. How can we stop the escalation of sensational, mindless content by the industry-generated culture if human brains are easily conditioned to seek it?

With the Vital Five, we grow young brains that can think and that can empathize. Children nurtured with the Vital Five will be less likely to want mindless stimulation or to choose violent or sensational entertainment.

6. How can parents meet their children's real human needs and their own human needs in a larger culture that avoids recognition of those needs?

Practice the Vital Five. The less attention we give to the industry-generated culture, the more attention we free up to give to our children.

A Clear Human Identity

In Chapter Two we discussed the importance of a clear parenting identity. Having a clear human identity is just as important. Understanding ourselves as essential and integral to the natural world, we perceive the industry-generated culture in new ways. It doesn't have to affect us or our children negatively. With the Vital Five keeping us on track, we move back into life processes and rhythms. By attending to what makes us more fully human, we find that positive changes in our children come from timely growth rather than from quick fixes and artificial remedies. Remembering our humanity and defining ourselves as humans can be fun as we see the spiraling outward of significant changes the more we attend to our real human needs. In a sense, all we have to do is re-frame how we think about ourselves in an industry-generated culture. We need to shine the spotlight on our own, and on our children's, humanity.

Innovative thinker Peter Senge reminds us that "the critical shifts required to guarantee a healthy world for our children and our children's children will not be achieved by doing more of the same…Nothing will change in the future without fundamentally new ways of thinking." [2] The Vital Five can be a fundamental new way of thinking. I often explain to parents about the value of leveraging. If we are so scattered and try to do a lot of things to help our kids, or if we are so stressed and don't know what to do about our children's "problems," we can end up burning ourselves out. In an industry-generated culture, many parents find that they put too much energy into parenting without enough rewards. It seems like that no matter what they do for their kids, it isn't enough. And in a way, that's true. If what we are doing isn't leveraged to meet core human needs, it's like always making the icing for the cake, but having no cake baked to put it on. The Vital Five bakes the cake.

If we lived in a culture created and maintained by people for people, it would be a lot easier to get our human needs met. But as it is, we, the parents in the culture, need to be very intentional about meeting them, for this provides the most direct way to cultivate a human identity. Many kids are growing up with a distorted sense of their humanity. Consider the fact that so many teens take on the images that are given to them through the industry-generated culture. If they were growing up with a clear human identity, they would have to struggle to separate their healthy sense of self from the distorted fantasy images they are sold. In fact, there would be an intense internal struggle not to succumb to the power of the images. But in our current culture, there is often little or no struggle at all. It's as if our kids' inner human identity is so fragile, it doesn't exist. Since so many teens embrace screen images and personally identity with them, industry-generated images become the core of their ego structure.

In her book *Branded: The Buying and Selling of Teenagers*, Alissa Quart tells of young girls with aneroxia, who call themselves "pro-anas." They consider their condition normal. Having found each other through the Internet, they are doing what young teens need to do: affirm their identity with others of their kind. Quart explains that "the pro-anas have taken the name of their malady and reclaimed it as a supposedly positive identity, even as a lifestyle...[but] what is most troubling about the pro-anas is that, like the teen cosmetic surgery girls and the boy bodybuilders, their identification with the disease now starts younger and younger. Ten percent of those who suffer from anorexia report the onset at ten years old or younger, and another 33 percent report the onset between ages eleven and fifteen." [3]

When industry-generated images fill children's heads and those children have not had the Vital Five met, the core, human identity will be distorted in some way. These kids are now emotionally attached to an externally manufactured ideal, redefining their humanity in relation to it. As Quart writes, "Pro-anas may be the most tragically victimized of all the branded kids of Generation Y. They're certainly the most interested in showing their wounds...Marketers have convinced these kids that they need a specific set of physical attributes, and that their own qualities must be obviated. For the large sub-cultures of teens who self-brand into look-alikes...the supposed freedom of self-creation is not a freedom at all. What they have is a consumer choice, no substitute for free will." [4]

While marketers do a great job of convincing kids of the need to look a certain way, meeting the Vital Five prevents this from happening. With these five essential needs met, children can grow up to know who they are. All of our children long to be fully human. As Rachel Naomi Remen writes, "Every acorn yearns toward the full expression of its nature and uses all opportunity to realize its capacity to become an oak tree. There is a natural yearning toward wholeness and wisdom in us all as well. This varies in strength from person to person. It may be quite conscious in some and deeply buried in others; it may form the focus of one life and lie on the periphery of another, but it is always there. Wholeness is a basic human need." [5]

With the Vital Five met our children can become whole people who know themselves to be fully human. This, in turn, would reshape our culture into a personally-generated one. We have no need for traditional revolutions, movements, or revolts against global enterprises. To get out from under industry control of our humanity, we must reclaim our humanity by meeting the Vital Five for our children. We then catalyze a personally-generated culture. When the elements (the people) in our living system are healthy and functioning at optimal capacity, then the people and the entire living system become creatively empowered. Sustained transformational cultural change begins with us parents.

Our Homes, Our Culture

The industry-generated culture definitely needs a strong parent. In many ways, it's like a child, out of control, forgetting the dignity of being human. We can't count on the industry-generated culture to grow up. We certainly can't take time away from our children to actively parent it. But what we can do is indirectly parent the industry-generated culture by parenting our children well. The extent to which our individual homes are personally-generated determines how quickly we move toward a personally-generated culture.

Germinating a personally-generated culture can be an exciting adventure. When we attend to the Vital Five, Vital Signs show up. Here are some of them:

We find ourselves having more energy.

Want to feel less tired and more optimistic? Watch less TV and turn it off when no one is watching. Using it as background noise can interfere with our energy levels. The constant blaring jars human nervous systems and makes it difficult for everyone in the family to concentrate. We expend valuable energy just dealing with the constant clatter. In their groundbreaking thirteen-year longitudinal study, Mihaly Csikszentmihalyi and Robert Kubey discovered some very interesting things about how adults felt after watching television. The more they watched, the less motivated they became. They felt more tired and drained after watching television than they did on jobs that they hated. Yet, once the stupor sets in, it's difficult to get out of it. It's as if in front of a TV, we humans forget how to pay attention to our real needs. [6]

With more attention to the Vital Five, however, and less time in front of screen machines, the body-mind is getting more of what it needs to renew itself. Renewal activities, like getting up and stretching after sitting for a time in front of a computer, or mustering up the energy to walk the dog after a tiring work day, actually increases our energy levels. We might have thought there was no way we could do yet another thing. But with a little push, we discover the benefits of energy renewing activities. It's delightful to feel more energy just when we thought we had depleted our source.

You'll find that the Vital Five give more vitality to you and your kids because with your core human needs met, you aren't expending extra energy trying to find substitutes. Each time something is done, either for yourself or for your child, that focuses on one or more of the Vital Five, you gain energy. It's like putting money in an interest-bearing savings account. Building an energy reserve for everyone in the family means more energy for fun activities together. Your collective creativity increases. This creates even more individual energy. Eventually more energy becomes available to reach out in our communities and serve.

Let's face it. Everything must start with energy. If we don't have the energy, we can't do a thing.

We feel more compassionate toward ourselves, other parents, and the industry-generated culture, in general.

With more energy, we increase our awareness. That awareness often leads to opening up our hearts. We see that as parents in an industry-generated culture we share commonalities with all parents. We are all doing the best we know how to do. As we meet our human needs, often we are more attuned to the humanness of others. We may find we become gentler with ourselves and more patient with others.

The word compassion literally means "with feeling." The Vital Five taps into our human nature to live from a place of authentic feeling and conviction. Compassion enables us to have empathy for others' feelings. We become less judgmental. Compassion brings with it more of a universal way to view our difficulties in parenting in an industry-generated culture. We are all in this together. We can assist and support one another.

With increased awareness and compassion, we don't have to set up the industry-generated culture to be the bad guy. We know it's currently part of the living system in which we all are parenting. The more human we become with the Vital Five, the more we can be centered in our relationship to the industry-generated culture.

We are less patient with industry-generated manipulations and screen images that berate, belittle, and demean all human potential. We feel a sense of urgency to bring more good into the world.

Trying to understand the industry-generated culture doesn't mean we accept its negative, anti-life messages. One of the greatest gifts of attending to the Vital Five is that by doing so, we implicitly give ourselves and our children permission to name dehumanizing industry-generated tactics and do something about them. Currently it seems that most U.S. adults are in some sort of unspoken conspiracy not to talk about or take action about the negative impact of screen machines in their lives. Sociologist Michael Lerner writes of a concept he calls "social unconscious," which he defines as "those shared meanings that most people assume in their daily interactions with others of which they are not aware and which they would resist knowing should they be pointed out." [7]

As more parents become more conscious of just how damaging the negative effects of screen machines and the industry-generated culture can be, more will talk and take action. And since more parents will see how they can alleviate some problems for their children and some of their own anguish by meeting the Vital Five, the urgency to move to a personally-generated culture will begin in earnest. A lot of times, though, we encounter an unavoidable process between feeling less patient to feeling more urgency. That process is a grief process.

When I speak to groups about how overuse and misuse of the home screen impacts children's brain development, inevitably some parents or educators will feel regret, shame, even guilt. Occasionally someone might leave the workshop halfway through, never to return, so overcome by uncomfortable feelings. A few call home during a break to make sure their baby-sitters, husbands, or wives, aren't letting the kids watch television.

I'm not trying to put fear or discomfort into parents. But once they truly understand the implications of the choices they make for their kids around screen technologies, pain, sometimes a lot of it, emerges. Recently, I tried to soothe a mother who called herself "stupid" after she viewed an educational video that showed violent video game content. She was shocked by their brutality, racism, and pornographic images. She worried that her kids may have played these games. I emphasized that she be gentle with herself. After all, we make decisions based on what we know. And she didn't know. That seemed to help, but her pain was intense. She was feeling what was lost to her children and to many children in our culture. And this loss is forever. We can't go back and repeat their childhood and "do it right." We did what we could, with what we knew at the time. That may bring some comfort, but it doesn't erase the pain.

Matthew Fox has written: "It is endemic to an unjust civilization to cover up the pain of its victims." [8] In a humane culture, we have room for true feelings of grief and remorse. From them will stem the urge to take effective actions in our homes and communities. After experiencing pain from injustice, we often find ourselves getting angry. The best remedy, of course, is action. Michael Learner gives us wise counsel:

> "Anger is positive when it is linked to action. Otherwise, it can wind in on itself, produce new levels of frustration, and become for some people an end in itself... To make our anger effective, we must learn to link our anger with each other's anger, see that we share a common set of problems and a common source of anger...anger when linked to action in this way, becomes a central part of any program for empowering people, undermining self-blaming, and creating social movements that can potentially change the world." [9]

We cultivate "boutique consciousness."

Nowadays, a lot of small boutiques aren't as expensive as super-mall department stores. Neighborhood boutiques often offer apparel and gift items, usually hand-made, for affordable prices. I love shopping in such places because the atmosphere is generally unhurried, the staff helpful, and the items special. Many boutiques hunt for treasures from other countries such as teak wooden gift boxes from Africa or 100% cotton lace linens from Ireland. Some specialize in items made by those in third-world nations, making sure that the people who put in the labor get paid their fair share.

Boutiques are more personal. A "boutique consciousness," then, is a way of living that celebrates the personal. For instance, I will go out of my way to find local artists who make beautiful things so I can give those as special gifts. I have a friend who makes exquisite pins and scarves and would much rather give her my business, because I would rather give the gift of her creative expression when I give gifts to my friends. Inevitably a gift like this evokes awe for the artist who designed it and a sense of wonder about the creativity of humans in general.

Writing in *The Power of Place*, Winifred Gallagher emphasizes, "If all the research on the best environments in which to raise and educate children could be boiled down to three words, they would be Small is Beautiful. Intimate surroundings, a low student-to-teacher ratio, neighborhood rather than regional facilities—these are the kinds of nongimmicky, less-is-more environmental influences that year after year have proved to foster both academic and social learning." [10] Small is not only beautiful where children are concerned, small is better. With the Vital Five we experience firsthand the tremendously energizing and freeing results the personal things we do bring to our children. And we notice that these are usually small things, done with a bit more deliberate purpose, perhaps, but small nevertheless. We may find ourselves playing more with our youngsters, as I described in my own experiences in Chapter Six. Or we may suddenly become aware that all the time we spent saying "No" to our child has finally resulted in him or her stopping to ask that nagging question. We are delighted to see that our child's attention is now on something different, and more in alignment with what we think best. In a lot of different ways like these, we see the small things paying off big time. With boutique consciousness we take ourselves and our parenting more seriously, bringing us a more light-hearted way of relating to our children—and ourselves.

We create personally-generated communities.

Business leader Robert Quinn calls them "productive communities." Episcopalian priest Matthew Fox calls them "base communities." The Commission for Children at Risk calls them "authoritative communities." Michael Lerner calls them "communities of meaning." In a wide variety of disciplines from diverse thinkers, many are coming up with the same conclusion: Small communities made up of caring adults are vital to our young and essential for a healthy culture. These communities share common characteristics:

- They nurture children and provide a structure for caring human bonds.
- They inspire participants to develop their full potential.
- They are multi-generational and encourage all voices to be expressed and heard.

- They instill the courage to take action against injustice of any kind.
- They cultivate human well-being as well as spiritual development.

As we gain energy, compassion, and develop a realistic relationship to the industry-generate culture and closer relationships in our families, we gain momentum to reach out to others. A personally-generated community can be as simple as a group of families getting together weekly for dinner. I know several families who do this. It means parents cooking a simple meal once a month, but three times a month they don't have to cook; they just show up. The families usually gather outside on someone's lawn in nice weather. It's fun. Enjoying adult camaraderie while their children play simple games together, parents share with each other and model a personally-generated community to their children.

Families talking with each other once a week in a neighborhood cul-de-sac may not seem significant. But it is. Such an activity embodies the definition of a community of meaning: "A community of people who share common values and goals, hopes and fears, symbols and rituals, give meaning and shape to the individual and family life." [11] As we meet the Vital Five in our homes, we have more time and energy for joining with like-minded parents. We can truly appreciate the value of such relationships because we aren't worn our struggling so much with industry-generated challenges. The Vital Five frees us to interact in meaningful ways with other parents to support each other in our parenting.

The trend back to more personal communities is growing on

many fronts. Smaller high schools are now recognized as being much better for kids not only for learning, but also for nurturing emotional well being. The proliferation of coffee houses and tea shops in major cities offer an intimate respite for personal conversations, places that weren't available a decade ago. More charter schools are being created, and Waldorf schools are the fastest growing segment of private schools in the country. Both stress personal, individualized attention to students. Small, organic farms are expanding. There is even a concept now called "slow food," countering the popular fast-food life style. Slow food means the food is selected and cooked with care. It's highly nutritious and you want to savor its many flavors. Slow food is ushering in more time for slow conversations.

Making the personal a priority means we attend to the Vital Five in our relationships and interactions. Sometimes our efforts at community-building get stymied. We may invite folks over for dessert and conversation and only one person shows up. Or we may find ourselves part of a community that has adopted the values of the industry-generated culture, and we have to speak out or leave that community. We may encounter well-intentioned parents that we have nothing in common with and can't see any reasons for getting together with them. One mother I met was so frustrated at trying to find like-minded parents when she moved to a new town that she ended up putting an ad in the paper. Meeting parents at her daughter's school or through the other usual routes didn't work. She met several mothers this way who shared her values and they have since created strong ties.

The people we hang out with most of the time should be people we love to be with, people who inspire us, support us, listen to us, and show us they care. Then we want to build relationships with them. A productive community emerges in this process. Communities can't be imposed on humans; rather they grow from inner felt needs. When we meet the Vital Five, a natural outcome is more intrinsic desire to be more deliberate in our living. That usually translates into forming more intentional relationships and communities.

What we do in our small, personally-generated communities is indeed profound. We link to our ancestors, spanning back thousands of years. What we do is what all human communities have done, and hopefully, will continue to do. In the elegant words of Michael Lerner, all communities share "important elements: a sense of what is right and wrong; a moral ordering of the universe within which any particular choice or situation could be evaluated; a set of rituals and symbols that could express the common understandings about the nature of the universe and one's place within it; a shared vocabulary for making sense of things; and a common agreement that people would support each other in creating a world that corresponded to these shared visions." [12]

Our Personal, Parenting Vision

Proverbs 29:18 says, "Where there is no vision, the people perish." It's a scary thought. I like to think, instead, "With a vision, the people thrive." What's your vision for yourself and for your children? If you could have the future the way you want it, what would it look like? What are you willing to do to make sure that future happens?

These are important questions for us to think about and talk about with our families and in our communities. Often in an industry-generated culture, we feel like we have to compete with mass produced images or projects with lots of money behind them. We don't get started because our efforts seem so insignificant in comparison. We may think: I can't come near a professionally-produced video, so why make one? I won't attract more than ten people to such a workshop, so why hold one? I don't have much money, so I can't take a chance. This type of self-talk negates the power of our personal dreams. In an industry-generated culture, it's easy to give up and walk away from an idea. But we have to help ourselves and each other not do this.

The industry-generated culture won't prompt us to take risks or seek answers. Dependent upon our insecurities to promote itself, such a culture can't nurture our attempts at self-expression. Essayist Rudolf Bahro has written, "When the forms of an old culture are dying, the new culture is created by a few people who are not afraid to be insecure." [12] Our feelings of not being confident do not have to stop us from making significant changes for ourselves, our children, or our communities.

The fundamental assumption of the industry-generated culture is that what's good for industry's bottom line is also good for people, that the toxicity poured forth is at "safe levels" and we and our children are not harmed by it. Nothing could be further from the truth. We and our children are being harmed. Therefore, we must remember that what we create personally has tremendous value. *Our personal creations are the only effective means to effectively counter the industry-generated culture.* Sure, what we create may not be polished. It may lack certain qualities. It won't be perfect. Being human, our personal contributions will be flawed. That's not only OK, but it's to be expected. The important thing is to take our responsibility to create seriously. After all, our real worth lies in our creative contributions. Mary Pipher writes in her moving book *The Shelter of Each Other* that the "definition of cultural wealth is...an ideal human culture...in which there is a place for every human gift."[13]

We can't create a more supportive culture for ourselves and our children without deeply valuing our unique, personal creations, because when we value them, we show that we value ourselves as well. Actually, everything we do or don't do is an act of self-creation. If we refuse to take our personal contributions seriously we may as well say to the industry-generated culture: "Make me and my children into whatever you want us to be."

Imagine a gardener who tills her soil, plants her seeds, and then scatters poison over the garden, saying to herself, "I wonder how much poison I can put on and still get the vegetables to grow?" Now imagine that she also plants weeds along with the vegetables, and waters and tends them as well, while saying to herself, "I wonder how many I can let grow there before they crowd out the vegetables?"

This scenario would only make sense as a scientific experiment to determine the effects of poison and weeds on a garden. But, in rational, sane behavior, this would only occur with a small trial garden—not for all the food we would depend on for the future. Our children *are* the future. Are we, as a society, unconsciously choosing to experiment with our children, to see how much poison and how many weeds they can cope with and still remain human?

Now imagine a gardener who tills her soil, plants her seeds, and then scatters some stuff over the garden that she has been given by distant experts, saying to herself, "I wonder if this really is poison? Some say it is, and some say it isn't. I don't know for sure. I hope it's not too bad for the garden. They said I was supposed to use it." Now imagine that she also plants weeds along with the vegetables, and waters and tends them as well, while saying to herself, "I wish I knew better how to tell which ones are really bad weeds, and which ones are probably OK. If I had more time and energy, I could probably find out, but I don't, so I guess the vegetables will just have to do the best they can."

In this situation of constrained choices, this gardener is like many of us parents —forced into making unsane choices. But we don't have to do that any longer. Supporting a vision toward new life means cultivating it carefully, making sure the environment is nurturing and life-enhancing. That's what makes sense. And that's what we do when we practice the Vital Five. Ultimately that's where our hopeful answers lie. Vacley Havel has said that hope is "not the conviction that something will turn out well, but the certainty that something makes sense regardless of how it turns out." [14] We can't have hope as parents without taking everyday actions that make sense. When we address the parenting challenges in an industry-generated culture through the Vital Five, we do what makes sense for our children and ourselves as human beings.

We then tap into the never-ending supply of wisdom within our own parenting wells. We clean up any toxicity we may find there from the industry-generated culture as best we can. From our parenting well we draw the courage to envision a personally-generated culture. And then, not knowing with certainty where the path will lead us or what the journey will be like, we begin moving toward our vision, knowing that we will join together with others to create the culture we want for our children and, for their children as well.

Notes

Introduction

1. *Epigraph.* Michael L. Umphrey, "Tinkling Cymbals and Sounding Brass: Hearing the Different Drum," paper presented to the Montana Education Association/Montana Federation of Teachers Annual Conference, (October 16, 2003), 5.

2. Bill O'Reilly, *Who's Looking Out for You?* (New York: Broadway Books, 2003), 16.

3. Kay S. Hymowitz, "The Contradictions of Parenting in a Media Age," in *Kid Stuff: Marketing Sex and Violence to America's Children*, edited by Diane Ravitch and Joseph P. Viteritti, (Baltimore: The John Hopkins University Press, 2003), 223.

4. Todd Gitlin, "Teaching amid the Torrent of Popular Culture," in *Kid Stuff: Marketing Sex and Violence to America's Children*, edited by Diane Ravitch and Joseph P. Viteritti, (Baltimore: The John Hopkins University Press, 2003), 20.

5. Henry A. Giroux, *Stealing Innocence: Corporate Culture's War on Children*, (New York: Palgrave, 2000), 4.

6. Gary Ruskin, "The Fast Food Trap: How Commercialism Creates Overweight Children," *Mothering*, (November/December 2003), 40.

7. Ibid.

8. Ibid.

9. Carol Rausch Albright and James B. Ashbrook, *Where God Lives in the Human Brain*, (Naperville: Sourcebooks, Inc., 2001), xxii.

10. Walter Wink, *Engaging the Powers: Discernment and Resistance in a World of Domination*, (Minneapolis: Fortress Press, 1992), 29.

11. Postman quote, "Social Critic and Educator Neil Postman Dies at 72," *NYU Today*, (October 24, 2003), Vol. 17, No. 3, 8.

Chapter 1: Today's Parenting Challenges

1. *Epigraph.* Ellen Goodman, Boston Globe columnist, quoted on Natural Family Online, http://www.naturalfamilyonline.com/advert/adprospectus.htm.

2. McKenna quote, *Ghosts from the Nursery: Tracing the Roots of Violence*, Robin Karr-Morse and Meredith S. Wiley, (New York: The Atlantic Monthly Press, 1997), 88.

3. Ibid.

4. *Webster's Ninth New Collegiate Dictionary*, 856.

5. Polly Berrien Berends, "Growing Together — While Growing Separately," *Spirituality & Health*, (Fall 1998), 15-17.

6. Judith L. Rubin, "No More Junk Toys: Rethinking Children's Gifts," *Mothering*, (November/December 2003), 47-48.

7. "The Troubling Arc of Media Concentration," *The Seattle Times*, March 31, 2004, B-10.

8. Charles Derber, *Corporation Nation*, (New York, St. Martin's Griffin, 1998), 4.

9. Ibid.

10. Rachel Eden, "Children's Creative Thinking in the Face of Commercialism," http://www.thepci.com/articles/eden_CreativeThinking.html.

11. Ibid.

12. Interview with Mary Burke, M. D., January 10, 2004.

13. Gary Ruskin, "The Fast Food Trap: How Commercialism Creates Overweight Children," *Mothering*, (November/December 2003), 40.

14. "Prevention of Pediatric Overweight and Obesity," *Pediatrics*, Vol. 112 No. (August 2003), 424-430.

15. Martha Miller, "Chubby Kids Have TV in Bedrooms," *Better Homes and Gardens*, (June 2002), 112.

16. Marcus Borg, *Meeting Jesus Again for the First Time*, (San Francisco: Harper San Francisco, 1994), 6.

17. Liza Mudy, "Do You Know Where Your Children Are? Most likely, they're watching PG-13 movies," The Washington Post, (Sunday, November 16, 2003), W-12.

18. Ibid.

19. Ibid.

20. Ibid.

21. Monica Eng, "The smell of success: Stink Blasters: Gassy toys are gross-out hits," *The Seattle Times*, (Nov. 16, 2003), L.-4.

22. Richard M. Ryan and Edward L. Deci, "Self-Determination Theory and the Facilitation of Intrinsic Motivation, Social Development, and Well Being," *American Psychologist*, (January 2000), 71.

23. Kay S. Hymowitz, "The Contradictions of Parenting in a Media Age," in *Kid Stuff: Marketing Sex and Violence to America's Children*, edited by Diane Ravitch and Joseph P. Viteritti, (Baltimore: The John Hopkins University Press, 2003), 228.

24. Ibid., 219.

25. American Academy of Pediatrics, Committee on Communications, "Children, Adolescents, and Television," *Pediatrics*, 1,119-1,120.

26. Robert Hill and Eduardo Castro, *Getting Rid of Ritalin: How Neurofeedback Can Successfully Treat Attention Deficit Disorder Without Drugs*, (Charlottesville, Hampton Roads Publishing Company, 2002), 151.

27. Craig A. Anderson, "Negative Effects of Violent Video Games," in *Kid Stuff: Marketing Sex and Violence to America's Children*, edited by Diane Ravitch and Joseph P. Viteritti, (Baltimore: The John Hopkins University Press, 2003), 152.

28. Zero to Three Public Policy Initiative, http://www.zerotothree.org/policy.

29. American Academy of Pediatrics, Committee on Communications, "Children, Adolescents, and Television," *Pediatrics*, 1,119-1,120.

30. James L. Baughman, *The Republic of Mass Culture: Journalism, Filmmaking and Broadcasting in America since 1941*, Second Edition, (Baltimore: The John Hopkins University Press, 1997), 236.

31. Katharine Heintz-Knowles, "The Reflection of the Screen: Television's Image of Children," *Children Now Study* (February, 1995): 5. and Kim Walsh Childers and Jane D. Brown, "Television Viewing and Adolescents' Belief About Male-Female Relationships," Association for Education in Journalism and Mass Communication Conference (10-13 August, 1989), 5.

32. Chris J. Boyatzis, "Of Power Rangers and V-Chips," *Young Children*, vol. 52 (November 1997), 75.

33. Emily Yearwood-Less, "Viciousness of youth attacks increases while numbers remain static," Canadian Press, (Sunday, December 7, 2003)

34. Matt Slagle, "Manhunt Redefines Video Game Violence," *Add Technology*, (Jan. 27, 2004), Associated Press.

35. Audrey M. Buchanan, et. al., "What Goes in Must Come Out: Children's Media Violence Consumption at Home and Aggressive behaviors at School," Paper presented at the International Society for the Study of Behavioral Development Conference, Ottawa, Ontario, Canada (August 2002).

36. Emily Yearwood-Less, "Viciousness of youth attacks increases while numbers remain static," Canadian Press, (Sunday, December 7, 2003).

37. Michael Medved, *Hollywood vs. America: Popular Culture and the War on Traditional Values*, (Harper Collins, 1994), 5.

38. Ibid., 4.

39. Reference to the book, *Carnival Culture: The Trashing of Taste in America*, James Twichwell, (Columbia University Press, 1992).

40. American Academy of Pediatrics, Committee on Communications, "Children, Adolescents, and Television," *Pediatrics*: 1,119-1,120.

41. Matthew Fox, *The Coming of the Cosmic Christ*, (Harper and Row Publishers, 1988), 40.

42. American Academy of Pediatrics, Committee on Communications, "Children, Adolescents, and Television," *Pediatrics*: 1,119-1,120.

43. Chris Christensen, paper presented to The Parent Coaching Institute for certification requirements, (October 2002).

44. Lawrence Diller, M.D., "Out of Whack," http://www.docdiller.com/article.php?sid=87.

Chapter 2: Reclaiming Our Parenting Identity

1. *Epigraph*. Erik H. Erikson, *Identity, Youth, and Crisis*, (New York: Norton, 1968), 127.

2. Mary Scribner, paper presented to The Parent Coaching Institute for certification requirements, (November 2003).

3. Jane Flagello, "Coaching and the 'Ah-Ha' Moment," in *Intentional Change*, John S. Stephenson, ed. (Xlibris Corporation, 1999), 66-67.

4. Gerald G. May, M.D., *Will and Spirit: A Contemplative Psychology*, (Harper and Row, 1983), 7.

5. Diane Ravitch and Joseph P. Viteritti, editors, *Kid Stuff: Marketing Sex and Violence to America's Children*, (The John Hopkins University Press, 2003), 13.

6. Susan Allport, *A Natural History of Parenting*, (Three Rivers Press, 1997), 27.

7. Marianne Williamson, *The Healing of America*, (Simon and Schuster, 1997), 249.

8. Margaret Wheatley, *Leadership and the New Science: Discovering Order in a Chaotic World*, (Brett-Koehler Publishers, 1999), 86.

9. Karen Bierdeman, written correspondence, December 30, 2003.

10. Kenneth Gergen, *The Saturated Self: Dilemmas Of Identity in Contemporary Life*, (Basic Books, 1991), 119-122.

11. Susan Byrnes, "It's about setting limits on the television set," *Seattle Times*, (November 11, 2003), B-4.

12. Leslie Mayer, paper presented to The Parent Coaching Institute for certification requirements, (September 2003).

13. Robert E. Quinn, *Change the World: How Ordinary People Can Accomplish Extraordinary Results*, (Jossey-Bass, Inc., 200), 78.

14. Ibid, 81.

15. Diane Dreher, personal correspondence, January 7, 2004.

Chapter 3: The First Essential Need: A Loving Parent-Child Bond

1. Thomas Lewis, M.D., Fari Amini, M.D., Richard Lannon, M.D., *A General Theory of Love*, (Vintage Books, 2000), viii.

2. John Condry, *The Psychology of Television*, (Lawrence Erlbaum Associates, 1989), 14.

3. Thomas Lickona, M.D., *Raising Good Children*, (Bantam Books, 1983).

4. Stephen Kline, *Out of the Garden: Toys, TV, and Children's Culture in an Age of Marketing*, (New York: Verso Books, 1995).

5. *The Coming of the Cosmic Christ*, 30.

6. Harold Bloom, *Global Brain: The Evolution of Mass Mind from the Big Bang to the 21st Century*, (New York, John Wiley & Sons, Inc, 2000), 7.

7. Daniel J. Siegel, *The Developing Mind: How Relationships and the Brain Interact to Shape Who We Are*, (New York, The Guilford Press, 1999), 72.

8. Anthony Stevens, *Archetypes: A Natural History of the Self*, (New York: William Morrow and Company, Inc., 1982), 119-121.

9. "Terminal Friendship," *The Guardian*, Association for the Supervision of Curriculum Development, February, 24, 2004.

10. Winifred Gallagher, *The Power of Place: How Our Surroundings Shape Our Thoughts, Emotions, and Actions*, (New York: Harper Collins), 110.

11. *A General Theory of Love*, 39.

12. Ibid., 36.

13. Ibid., 23.

14. *The Power of Place*, 110.

15. *Global Brain*, 154.

16. Bruce Perry, M.D., "Incubated in Terror: Neurodevelopmental Factors in the 'Cycle of Violence,'" in *Children in a Violent Society*, Joy D. Osofsky, ed. (New York: The Guilford Press, 1997), 124-129.

17. *A General Theory of Love*, 156.

18. *The Developing Mind*, 226.

19. Ibid., 30.

20. Carla Hannaford, *Smart Moves: Why Learning is Not All in Your Head*, (Arlington: Great Ocean Publishers, 1995), 25-26.

21. Ibid., 84.

22. Ramey quote, *Inside the Brain: Revolutionary Discoveries of How the Mind Works*, Ronald Kotulak, (Kansas City, Andrews McMeel Publishing, 1996), 52.

23. *The Power of Place*, 156-157.

24. *Ghosts from the Nursery*, 293.

25. quoted in *Stop Teaching Our Kids to Kill: A Call to Action Against TV, Movie, and Video Game Violence*, Lt. Co. Dave Grossman and Gloria DeGaetano, (New York: Crown, 1999), 56.

26. Louise Barbee, personal interview, February 19, 2004.

27. Ibid.

28. Erich Fromm, *The Art of Loving*, (New York, Perennial Reprint, 2000).

29. Alanna Mitchell, "Unglued," *Globe and Mail*, (January 31, 2004), C-8.

30. Meredith F. Small, "Family Matters," *Discover Magazine*, (August 2000), 68-69.

31. Alanna Mitchell, "Unglued."

32. Mary Burke, M. D., "The Slime Oozing out of the TV Set: Television and the Developing Brain," Paper presented to the Department of Psychiatry, Langley Porter Psychiatric Institute, University Of California, San Francisco, 2004, 3.

33. Barbara Strauch, *The Primal Teen: What the New Discoveries About the Teenage Brain Tell Us About Our Kids*, (New York: Doubleday, 2003), 136.

34. Diane Dreher, personal interview, January 10, 2004.

35. C. R. Synder, Diane McDermott, William Cook, Michael Rapoff, *Hope for the Journey: Helping Children Through Good Times and Bad*, (New York: Westview Press, 1997), xiii.

36. Ibid., 7.

Chapter 4: The Second Essential Need: An Interior Life

1. *Epigraph*. Matthew Fox, *The Re-Invention of Work: A New Vision of Livelihood for Our Time*, (New York: Harper Collins, 1994), 22.

2. Jacob Needleman, *Money and the Meaning of Life*, (New York: Currency, 1994), 54.

3. Buscaglia quote, Margaret Storz in "Real Self-Love," *Science of Mind Magazine*, (February, 2004), 52.

4. *Hope for the Journey: Helping Children Through Good Times and Bad*, 10.

5. Mihaly Csikszentmihalyi, *Flow: The Psychology of Optimal Experience*, (New York, Harper & Row, 1990), 127.

6. *The Power of Place*, 157.

7. Ibid., 157-159.

8. Kevin Bogle, "What is the Effect of Television and Radio on Reading Performance," Classen School of Advanced Studies, (Oklahoma City, Fall, 2003).

9. Anneli Rufus, *Party of One: The Loner's Manifesto*, (New York: Marlowe and Company, 2003), 267.

10. Ibid, 257.

11. Alfie Kohn, *Punished by Rewards*, (Boston: Houghton Mifflin, 1993), 146.

12. Ibid.

13. Richard M. Ryan and Edward L. Deci, "Self-Determination Theory and the Facilitation of Intrinsic Motivation."

14. Research conducted by Debra Pepler, LeMarsh Centre for Research on Violence and Conflict Resolution, York University, 1997, cited in pamphlet distributed by www.bullying.org.

15. Amanda Paulson (The Christian Science Monitor), "Bullies: Vicious and Wired," in *The Seattle Times*, (February 23, 2004), C-2

16. Debra J. Pepler and Wendy Craig, "Making a Difference in Bullying," Report, #60, Queens's College, 1988, 5.

Chapter 5: The Third Essential Need: Image Making

1. *Epigraph*. Kenneth E. Boulding, *The Image: Knowledge in Life and Society*, (Ann Arbor: University of Michigan Press, 1997), 25.

2. Antonio Damasio, *The Feeling of What Happens: Body and Emotion in the Making of Consciousness*, (New York: Harcourt Brace and Company, 1999), 318.

3. Joseph Chilton Pearce. *Evolution's End: Claiming the Potential of Our Intelligence*, (San Francisco: Harper & Row, 1992), 68.

4. Ibid.

5. *Flow: The Psychology of Optimal Experience*, 128.

6. Ibid.

7. Ibid.

8. *Evolution's End: Claiming the Potential of Our Intelligence*, 165-166.

9. Ibid., 167-168.

10. Jeffrey Scheuer, *The Sound Bite Society: Television and the American Mind*, (New York: Four Walls Eight Windows, 1999), 72.

11. Terrence W. Deacon, *The Symbolic Species: The Co-Evolution of Language and the Brain*, (New York, W. W. Norton & Company, 1997), 413.

12. Dorothy G. Singer, Jerome L. Singer, Sharon L. Plaskon, and Amanda E. Schweder, "A Role for Play in the Preschool Curriculum," in *All Work and No Play: How Educational Reforms are Harming Our Preschoolers*, edited by Sharna Olfman, (Westport: Prager Publishers, 2003) 44.

13. Bruner quote, *Television and the Lives of Our Children*, Gloria DeGaetano (Redmond: Train of Thought Publishing, 1993), 24.

14. Wendy Josephson, *Television Violence: A Review of the Effects on Children of Different Ages*, Ottawa: A National Clearinghouse on Family Violence, 1995, 54.

15. Joseph LeDoux, *Synaptic Self: How Our Brains Become Who We Are*, (New York: Penguin Books, 2002), 322.

16. Erik H. Erickson, *Childhood and Society*, (Chicago: Peter Smith Publishing, 2001).

17. Joanne Cantor, *Mommy I'm Sacred, How TV and Movies Frighten Children and What We Can Do To Protect Them*, (New York: Harcourt, Brace, and Company, 1998), 82-83.

18. Ibid., 84.

19. David L. Cooperrider, Diana Whitney, Jacqueline M. Stavros, *Appreciative Inquiry Handbook: The First in a Series of AI Workbooks for Leaders of Change*, (Bedford Heights: Lakeshore Publishers, 2003), 370.

20. Thomas Berry quote, *One River, Many Wells*, Matthew Fox, (New York: Jeremy P. Tarcher/Putnam, 2000), 301.

21. Imagination and Middle School Reform, http://www.middleweb.com/HMcreativity.html.

22. *Appreciative Inquiry Handbook: The First in a Series of AI Workbooks for Leaders of Change*, 374.

23. Ibid.

24. Ibid.

25. Ibid. p. 379.

26. Ibid.

Chapter 6: The Fourth Essential Need: Creative Expression

1. *Epigraph.* Mihaly Csikszentmihalyi, *Creativity: Flow and the Psychology of Discovery and Invention*, (New York: Harper Collins Publishers, 1996), 349.

2. Frances Prose, *The Lives of the Muses*, (New York: Harper Collins, 2002), 2.

3. Matthew Fox, *Creativity: Where the Divine and the Human Meet*, (New York: Jeremy Tarcher/Putnam), 59-60.

4. e. e. cummings quote, "Spiritual Growth," Don Welsh, *Science of Mind Magazine*, March 2004, 61.

5. Keen quote, *Sins of the Spirit, Blessings of the Flesh: Lessons for Transforming Evil in Soul and Society*, Matthew Fox, (New York: Three Rivers Press, 1999), 175.

6. Ellis Paul Torrance, *Creativity and Learning* (New York: Harper Collins, 1970).

7. Sherry Turkle, *The Second Self: Computers and the Human Spirit*, (New York: Simon and Schuster, 1984), 82.

8. *Evolution's End*, 106.

9. *Flow: The Psychology of Optimal Experience*, 85-86.

10. Mary McGee, *On Television: Teach the Children*, (San Francisco: California Newsreel, 1991).

11. *The Second Self*, 82-83.

12. *Flow: The Psychology of Optimal Experience*, 87.

13. *Creativity: Flow and the Psychology of Discovery and Invention*, 328.

14. Ibid.

15. Ibid., 327-328.

16. Ibid., 342.

17. Renate Nummela Caine and Geoffrey Caine, *Education on the Edge of Possibility*, (Alexandria: Association for the Supervision and Curriculum Development, 1997), 18.

18. Ibid., 153.

19. *One River, Many Wells*, 420.

Chapter 7: The Fifth Essential Need: Contribution as Relationship

1. *Epigraph.* Joan Borysenko, *A Woman's Book of Life: The Biology, Psychology, and Spirituality of the Feminine Life Cycle,* (Riverhead Books), 1996, 162.

2. *The Developing Mind,* p. 155.

3. Nancy M. Better, "How Long a Drive? *Finding Nemo* or *Harry Potter?*" *The New York Times,* November 21, 2003, http://nytimes.com/2003/11/21/automobiles/21KIDS.html.

4. Renate Nummela Caine and Geoffrey Caine, *Unleashing the Power of Perceptual Change,* (Alexandria: Association for Supervision and Curriculum Development, 1997), 102.

5. Ibid.

6. Ibid.

7. Ibid., 103.

8. Rachel Naomi Remen, *My Grandfather's Blessings,* (New York: Riverhead Books, 2001), 97.

9. Ibid.

10. Michael Lerner, *Surplus Powerlessness,* (Oakland: The Institute for Labor & Mental Health, 1986), 88-89.

11. "Hardwired to Connect: The New Scientific Case for Authoritative Communities," The Commission on Children at Risk, (September 2003), 4.

12. Ibid., 2.

13. Ibid.

14. Ann Katherine Bradley, "In Search of Unlimited Love," *Science of the Mind Magazine,* (June 2003), 17-18.

15. Ibid.

16. Ibid., 14.

17. Jennifer LaGuardia and Richard Ryan, "What Adolescents Need: A Self-Determination Theory Perspective on Development with Families, School, and Society," in *Academic Motivation of Adolescents,* edited by Frank Pajares and Tim Urdan, (Greenwich: Information Age Publishing, 2003), 195.

18. Bonnie Benard research cited http://www.wested.org/cs/we/view/rs/712.

19. *The Saturated Self,* 239.

20. Mikela Tarlow, *Navigating the Future,* (New York: McGraw Hill, 1999), 208.

21. "Overcoming Lack of Motivation for Learning," *Kappan Magazine*, (March 2004), http://www.pdkintl.org/kappan/k0403rob.htm.

22. Denise Bolger Kovnat, "Interior Motives, *Rochester Review*, (Spring 2001), 4.

23. Ibid., 5-6.

24. Ryan and Deci, 70-71.

25. Alan Atkinson, paper presented to the Parent Coaching Institute for certification requirements, June 2003.

26. Robert K. Greenleaf, *Servant Leadership: A Journey into the Nature of Legitimate Power and Greatness*, (New York: Paulist Press, 1977), 13.

27. Ibid.

Chapter 8 : Toward a Personally-Generated Culture

1. *Epigraph.* Jim Dator, quoted in Public Education Network Newsletter, Spring 2003.

2. Senge quote in *Unleashing the Power of Perceptual Change*, 14.

3. Alissa Quart, *Branded: The Buying and Selling of Teenagers*, (New York: Basic Books, 2003), 140-141.

4. Ibid., 142.

5. *My Grandfather's Blessings*, 82.

6. Mihaly Csikszentmihalyi and Robert Kubey, *Television and the Quality of Life: How Everyday Viewing Shapes Everyday Experiences*, (Hillsdale: Lawrence Erlbaum Associates, 1990).

7. *Surplus Powerlessness*, 12.

8. *The Re-Invention of Work*, 32.

9. *Surplus Powerlessness*, 160.

10. *The Power of Place*, 159.

11. *Surplus Powerlessness*, 92.

12. Bahro quote, "From Hope to Hopelessness," Margaret Wheatley, Writings, 2002, p. 1, www.margaretwheatley.com.

13. Mary Pipher, *The Shelter of Each Other: Rebuilding Our Families*, (New York: Putnman, 1996), 257.

14. Havel quote, "From Hope to Hopelessness," Margaret Wheatley, Writings, 2002, p. 1, www.margaretwheatley.com.

About the Author

Gloria DeGaetano is a best-selling author, popular speaker, and the founder and CEO of The Parent Coaching Institute. The Parent Coaching Institute offers parent coaching services to parents nationwide, along with a graduate training program for educators and counselors wanting to become certified parent coaches. To learn more, please visit www.thepci.com.